W9-BYB-617

must-see
VENICE

CONTENTS

Published by Thomas Cook Publishing
A division of Thomas Cook Holdings Ltd
PO Box 227, Thorpe Wood
Peterborough PE3 6PU
United Kingdom

Telephone: 01733 503571
E-mail: books@thomascook.com

Text: © 2000 Thomas Cook Publishing
Maps: © 2000 Thomas Cook Publishing

ISBN 1 841570 75 3

Distributed in the United States of America by the Globe Pequot Press,
PO Box 480, Guilford, Connecticut 06437, USA.

Distributed in Canada by Whitecap Books, 351 Lynn Avenue,
North Vancouver, British Columbia, Canada V7J 2C4.

Distributed in Australia and New Zealand by Peribo Pty Limited,
58 Beaumont Road, Mt Kuring-Gai, NSW, 2080, Australia.

Publisher: Stephen York
Commissioning Editor: Deborah Parker
Map Editor: Bernard Horton

Series Editor: Christopher Catling

Written and researched by: Teresa Fisher

All rights reserved. No part of this publication may be reproduced, stored in
a retrieval system or transmitted, in any form or by any means, electronic,
mechanical, recording or otherwise, in any part of the world, without the prior
permission of the publishers. All requests for permission should be made to
the Publisher at the above address.

Although every care has been taken in compiling this publication, and the
contents are believed to be correct at the time of printing, Thomas Cook
Holdings Ltd cannot accept responsibility for errors or omissions, however
caused, or for changes in details given in the guidebook, or for the consequences
of any reliance on the information provided.

The opinions and assessments expressed in this book do not necessarily
represent those of Thomas Cook Holdings Ltd.

Readers are asked to remember that attractions and establishments may open,
close or change owners or circumstances during the lifetime of this edition.
Descriptions and assessments are given in good faith but are based on the
author's views and experience at the time of writing and therefore contain
an element of subjective opinion which may not accord with the reader's
subsequent experience. We would be grateful to be told of any changes or
inaccuracies in order to update future editions. Please notify them to the
Commissioning Editor at the above address.

Cover photograph: John Heseltine

must-see VENICE

TERESA FISHER

Getting to know Venice

Discovering Venice

'Streets flooded. Please advise', wrote Robert Benchley in a telegram on arrival in Venice. And it's true. Even though Venice has been painted, described and filmed more than any city in the world, nothing can prepare you for that first, powerful impact – however it happens. Whether you are in a gondola on the Grand Canal when the city is enveloped in the mists of winter, or watching the setting of the summer sun bathe the city in the magical colours which inspired such artists as Titian, Veronese and Canaletto, your first impressions will be memorable.

For centuries, both Venetians and visitors have been spellbound by this most extraordinary floating city, equal parts stone and water; a unique and breathtakingly beautiful man-made metropolis ingeniously built on 200 tiny islands, with 'the sea for its floor, the sky for its roof, and the flow of water for walls' (Boncompagno da Signa, 1240); the historic flagship of a mighty fleet of islands in the lagoon; the most photogenic city in the world.

Few cities can boast such artistic richness. As the gateway to the Orient, and under the leadership of the doge for many centuries, the city ruled as a **world capital** and a **mighty sea power**. Its immense wealth was celebrated in art and architecture throughout the city. Nowadays, with the glories of this heritage evident at every turn, you could easily mistake Venice for a painting come alive, a stage-set full of real people, an open-air museum.

Venice, however, is no museum. It is a living, fragile city of ageing *palazzi*, flaking façades and ominously tilting bell-towers, standing testimony to the city's ephemerality, a constant reminder of a pending watery grave. Yet despite its decaying foundations, the encroaching water and rising silt, Venice is a delicate miracle of survival, although it is by no means free from problems. Along with mounting concerns about increasing levels of pollution from nearby industrial towns, which are irreparably corroding the city's ancient stonework, the population is continuing to dwindle as modern houses, jobs and other attempts to preserve Venice for the Venetians clash with those aimed at preserving the city for posterity.

Venice's must-see landmarks (or should one say 'watermarks'?) – including, of course, **St Mark's Basilica**, the **Doge's Palace**, the **Rialto Bridge** and the water-lapped *palazzi* of the Grand Canal – are delightfully idiosyncratic, blending Renaissance, Gothic and Byzantine styles. But when we leave Venice, our memories will not only be of its beauty and art treasures but also of city life: pasta *al fresco* in a peaceful, sun-splashed piazza; the sluggish, green backwaters; the dancing of gondolas tied to gaily striped mooring poles; buildings reflected in the still waters of the canals; the sights and scents of local markets; shop windows brimming with carnival masks and dazzling glass displays; even St Mark's Square flooded on a high tide.

For this is the magic of Venice, which entices devoted visitors back year after year to La Serenissima – 'the most serene' and captivating city in the world.

Life in Venice

Venetians are passionate about Venice – its slow pace of life, its shimmering light, its magnificent monuments and its unique watery character. Like Marco Polo, they are victims of true Italian campanilismo *– an enduring attachment to their roots. This deep civic pride results in a* **clean, efficiently run city** *distinguished by little crime and an extraordinary tolerance of the myriad tourists who invade their city 365 days of the year.*

Like the sea which surrounds them, Venetians are often characterised as being cold and contradictory. Their mercurial moods are likened to the tide – 'six hours up and six hours down', according to a Venetian proverb. In fact, they are a **loyal, relaxed, fun-loving people** – qualities reflected in their love of carnival and pageantry – who always have time for a chat, a coffee in a neighbourhood café or an *ombra* (a small glass of wine) in a local bar. But at the same time they are **cool and conservative**, their philosophical detachment often mistaken for aloofness. Historically, they were revered (and feared a little) throughout Italy for their autonomous approach and mercantile prowess, and long admired for their refined, discerning taste, smug within their city of unrivalled musical and artistic heritage.

A dying breed

True Venetians are a dying breed. Their numbers are sapped by emigration *di là dall'acqua* ('over the water') to mainland Mestre, and the remaining population is aged. Yet the decline is in numbers rather than spirit, as they fight the straitjacket of tourism. They don't want to live in a museum world of picture-postcards, tourist menus and plastic souvenirs, they want to maintain a 'living' city of true Venetian values, and have even preserved their dialect, Venessian, which acts as a strong bond between locals.

Practicalities

When it comes to practicalities, all the trappings of normal life end in **Piazzale Roma**, the terminus of the city's sole road. From this point, everything has to be delivered by boat or on foot, and, although the city is only roughly the size of New York's Central Park, there are over 44km (27 miles) of canals and over 200km (125 miles) of alleyways to navigate.

Aspects of city life we take for granted – carrying heavy shopping, moving house (by boat!), rubbish collections (with ingenious barges which use lifts), pushing prams (over 400 bridges!) – don't apply in Venice. There's no smog or heavy traffic either, but what about those devastating floods (nobody sleeps on the ground floor), or the risk of toddlers falling into the canals? As Bruno Barilli commented in *Lo Stivale*: 'Here everyone goes on foot, walking close to the house walls to avoid falling into the water.'

Venice at play

But life's not all tough in Venice. True Venetians are hearty outdoors folk, out on the water in summer and on the nearby ski slopes in winter. With the seaside resort of the Lido right on the doorstep and the Dolomites just an hour away by car, a true Venetian family owns a car and a boat and probably has a small holiday residence in the countryside. Even Venetians sometimes enjoy being on 'terra firma'!

Yesterday and tomorrow

It is thought that the first real inhabitants were refugees who fled from the plains of northern Italy during the barbarian invasions of the fifth and sixth centuries. Over the centuries their small settlements grew until they coalesced into a single city – Civitas Venetiarum – *which, to mark its independence and prestige, elected a single leader, the* **doge**, *and stole the body of* **St Mark** *from Alexandria as its patron saint.*

A rising power

From 726 to 1797, Venice was ruled by a series of 120 doges who, during the city's most formative years, enjoyed almost unlimited powers. Following tentative gains in the Adriatic during the early Middle Ages, and culminating in the conquest of Byzantium in 1204, Venice became the leading maritime power in the Mediterranean. Before long, she boasted the **largest empire in the Western world**, and was one of the wealthiest cities in Europe – La Serenissima, the glorious Venetian Republic. Trade with the East was the main source of her power and wealth, and the Eastern connection has left its mark today in the glut of Byzantine-influenced art and architecture.

> ❝ *Venice was founded in misfortune … the early chronology is hazy and debatable, and nobody really knows what happened when.* ❞
>
> **Jan Morris,** *Venice,* **1960**

The fall of the Republic

No enemy in the Republic's 1 000-year history ever succeeded in taking Venice by storm. However, Venice's subsequent decline in fortune – mainly due to declining trade, the rise of

the Turks, the emergence of the New World and the combined forces of other European countries – eventually reduced the city from world power to provincial backwater status. No longer a major player on the world stage, Venice became Europe's decadent playground during the seventeenth and eighteenth centuries, with the emergence of coffee houses, the first public gaming houses and the sumptuous **La Fenice opera house**.

By 1797, the city was quite powerless to resist the inexorable rise of France and **Napoleon**, who took control of the city, demolishing over 50 churches and 40 palaces and deliberately wrecking the shipyards of the Arsenale as a sign of his contempt for the Republic. Following Napoleon's defeat at Waterloo in 1815, the city surrendered to Austria for the next half a century until liberation, and subsequent integration with a united Italy, came in 1866.

Looking to the future

Venice survived the world wars of the twentieth century surprisingly unscathed. It was only during the post-war industrial boom, with the development of the sprawling mainland factories at **Marghera**, that the Venetians drew a question mark over the future of their city by compounding its growing problems of pollution with those of depopulation and urban decay (*see page 35*), not to mention the eternal, relentless and corrosive advance of the sea (*see pages 108–9*). As a result, the main choice facing the city nowadays is whether to preserve Venice for the Venetians (by providing modern houses, more jobs and better communications) or to forgo its status as a living metropolis and preserve it for posterity, as a life-sized museum-cum-theme park for tourists.

People and places

The city has always had a magnetic appeal for visitors, who are drawn by the glories of its art, architecture and music. Countless photographs and canvases (see pages 82–3) have been produced to immortalise its magic, and rivers of words have been written to describe it – but not always positively. D H Lawrence called it an 'abhorrent, green, slippery city', while Boris Pasternak found Venice 'swelling like a biscuit soaked in tea'.

Literary Venice

Through the centuries, Venice has attracted an extraordinary range of writers, from Goethe, Petrarch and Shakespeare (who never visited the city but vividly portrayed it in *The Merchant of Venice* and *Othello*) to Proust, James and Mann. As so little has changed in the city, their words still have a powerful impact today. The carnivals, balls and fun-loving society also attracted the Romantics, such as Wordsworth, Shelley and Byron, all of whom addressed poems to the city.

Venice has surprisingly few home-grown writers, apart from Marco Polo, Casanova and Carlo Goldoni, with only the latter famous principally for his literary works. Marco Polo is, of course, better known for his thirteenth-century voyages of discovery in the Far East than for his great oeuvre, the *Description of the World* – for a long time regarded as Europe's most accurate account of the East – and Giacomo Casanova is celebrated more as Italy's greatest lover than for his voluminous memoirs.

Musical Venice

Visually, Venice may be enchanting, her art and architecture among the finest achievements of Western civilisation, but the city has also been the centre of European musical life from the High Renaissance to the age of baroque. **Gabrieli**, **Monteverdi**, **Vivaldi** and countless other composers worked here to feed the voracious appetite for spectacle which so distinguished Venetian public life. Antonio Vivaldi was born here in 1678 and, as concert-master of La Pietà, composed many of his finest concertos for the church, including the celebrated *Four Seasons* (*see page 116*). In the nineteenth century, the great romantic composers **Wagner**, **Verdi** and **Rossini** took inspiration from the city.

All at sea

Many celebrities have found themselves actually *in* the canals rather than beside them. **George Eliot**'s honeymoon was ruined when her husband fell off a hotel balcony into the Grand Canal and nearly died. **Byron** would frequently swim down the Grand Canal to the Lido. A great eccentric, his household comprised a fox, a wolf, cats, dogs and monkeys, not to mention various mistresses, including *La Fornarina* ('the little oven' – the wife of a baker), who, having been banished from the *palazzo*, once attacked Byron with a knife and threw herself into the canal. More recently, **Katharine Hepburn** fell into Canal San Barnaba in Dorsoduro while filming *Midsummer Madness*, suffering permanent damage to her eyesight.

Film-set Venice

Venice has certainly made its mark around the world on celluloid as the setting of countless films, including *Death in Venice, Don't Look Now, Portrait of a Lady, Wings of the Dove, Othello* and *Indiana Jones and the Last Crusade*.

Getting around

The *sestieri*

Merely terrestrial cities may be divided into any number of quarters, but watery Venice is divided into sixths (*sestieri*): Cannaregio, Santa Croce, San Polo, Dorsoduro, San Marco and Castello. Most of the major sights are within San Marco (**St Mark's Basilica**, **St Mark's Square**, the **Doge's Palace**), San Polo (**Rialto Bridge** and **markets**) and Dorsoduro (the **Accademia** and **Peggy Guggenheim Museum**), while Santa Croce and Cannaregio are the least touristic, containing some of the city's most beautiful canals.

Although compact, Venice is a veritable maze, with its countless *calli* (alleys) and *campi* (squares). The Grand Canal is a good point of reference. It sweeps through the heart of the city in an inverted S-shape, and big yellow signposts indicate the way to the main sights, but on finding some of the lesser attractions you will invariably come across numerous routes ending at a canal, with no bridge across to the other side. So, before you start exploring the city, make sure you get a good map.

" *Nothing is simpler than to lose oneself in Venice; and nothing is more fun than to be in this labyrinth without a Minotaur, as a Theseus without an Ariadne's thread!* "
Jean-Louis Vaudoyer

Guided tours

Tours of Venice with English-speaking guides can be booked through many travel agencies, including American Express (*Salizzada San Moisè 1471, San Marco; tel: 041 5200844*) and World Vision Travel (*Campiello della Feltrina 2513a, San Marco; tel: 041 5230933*).

Public transport

Public transport is surprisingly straightforward in Venice. You go by water everywhere, and where you cannot, you must walk. Comfortable shoes are a must!

To travel by boat, there are a variety of options. *Vaporetti* (water-buses) run the length of the Grand Canal, circle the city and also operate to the outlying islands. Fares are cheap, and they also offer some of the best views. Water-taxis will take you wherever you wish, but at a price! The minimum fare is roughly equivalent to a full week's pass for the *vaporetti* and will just about get you across the Grand Canal. A cheaper, more entertaining way to cross the canal is by *traghetto* (gondola-ferry), and then, of course, there's the real thing: the ride of a lifetime in a **gondola**.

Vaporetti

The *vaporetto,* or water-bus, is the principal means of transport, operated by the public transport system, ACTV. The main routes run every 10 to 20 minutes during the day. Services are reduced in the evening, especially after midnight. Some of the routes are served by smaller, faster boats called *motoscafi*, and there are also large two-tier *motonavi*, which serve the Lido and other outlying islands.

Details of routes and timetables are situated at every landing-stage. Alternatively, give ACTV a call (*041 5287886*) for information. Tickets are available at most landing-stages, some bars, shops and tobacconists displaying the ACTV sign. The price of a ticket remains the same whether you are going one stop or doing an entire circuit, but some routes are more expensive than others. The fast *diretto* boats charge more than those which stop at every landing-stage.

Here are some useful *vaporetto* routes:

No 1: Confusingly called the *accelerato,* this is the slow boat down the Grand Canal and on to the Lido.

No 82: A faster route down the Grand Canal, from Tronchetto to San Zaccaria and, in summer, to the Lido.

Nos 51/52 and 41/42: These routes skirt the periphery of Venice, 41/42 in a clockwise direction and 51/52 in an anti-clockwise direction. Although they are called *circolare*, to go right round the city you will have to change boats at Fondamente Nuove. No 41/42 also includes Murano in its circuit.

No 12: The main route to Murano, Burano and Torcello.

Water-taxis

Water-taxis are the best mode of transport for those with little time and sufficient finances. They can be hired from 16 water-taxi ranks, including one at the airport, the railway station, Piazzale Roma, San Marco and the Lido. They can also be ordered by telephone (*041 5229750 or 041 5222303*). Fares are regulated by a tariff, with supplements charged for luggage and night services, but beware: some will try to charge you

considerably more than the official fare. Be sure to agree the price *before* boarding.

Traghetti

Gondola-ferries – *traghetti* – cross the Grand Canal between special piers at seven different points, providing a vital service for pedestrians. They are indicated by yellow street signs illustrated with a tiny gondola symbol. The very reasonable fare is paid to the gondolier on embarkation. Once aboard, do as the Venetians do – stay standing for the duration of the crossing.

Gondolas

The legendary Venetian gondola is undoubtedly the most enjoyable means of transport, but also the most expensive. Fares are governed by a tariff with a surcharge for night trips after 2 000 hours, but, as gondoliers are notorious for overcharging, it is often easiest to establish terms (cost and duration) by ordering a gondola via your tour representative or hotel staff. For a truly memorable outing, consider a two-hour gondola ride and take a picnic supper on board with you. Or, in summer, a gondola 'cruise'

– a flotilla of tourist-laden gondolas entertained by singers – provides a fun way to explore the waterways at an affordable price.

Travel passes

Rather than buy individual tickets for each *vaporetto* trip, it is usually more economical to opt for a travel pass. If you intend to make six or more journeys in a day, buy a **24-hour ticket** (*biglietto turistico*) – also available as a family travel card for groups of three, four or five people; if you plan to do ten or more trips within three days, buy a **72-hour ticket** Alternatively, purchase a *blocchetta* of ten or more tickets, which can be used over any period. All tickets must be date-stamped by the automatic machine on each pier before boarding. There is a supplementary charge – usually another full fare – for baggage other than hand luggage. If you stay longer, you can save money by purchasing a **weekly or monthly** *abbonamento* from any main ACTV ticket office. Holders of an International Student ID card can purchase a Rolling Venice card from the Tourist Office which, alongside discounts on certain hotels, theatres, shops and restaurants, provides concessions on travel, including a special three-day youth pass – the *Tre Giorni Giovane*.

Exploring the mainland

The best way to explore the mainland is either by car or by train. The leading international car rental companies have offices at Marco Polo airport and in Piazzale Roma. Parking, however, is a nightmare. All roads to Venice end at the monstrous municipal car parks of Piazzale Roma and its cheaper annex, Tronchetto – the largest car park in Europe. Parking here is moderately expensive per day, but reduces in cost for longer stays.

Travelling by train, on the other hand, is a cheap, easy and efficient way to see many of the key sights. Get rail information beforehand (*tel: 1478 88088*) or call into the helpful **information office at Santa Lucia station**. One of the best aspects of daily excursioning by train is the homeward-bound trip into Venice, right to the very edge of the Grand Canal. As Thomas Mann remarked, 'To enter Venice by train is like entering a palace by the back door.'

Don't miss

1 Accademia

The glory that once was Venice lives on in this dazzling collection of paintings spanning the thirteenth to the eighteenth centuries. From **Veneziano** to **Veronese**, **Tintoretto** to **Tiepolo**, the city's main art gallery is an absolute must (*see pages 68–71*).

2 Basilica San Marco

The magnificent gilded interior and mosaics of St Mark's Basilica, the city's cathedral, the 'Church of Gold' and one of the world's most richly embellished churches, lingers long in one's memory (*see pages 88–91*).

3 Backstreet Venice

Get lost amid the city's picture-book backwaters, or take to the water, ideally by gondola, to see the secret side of Venice, only accessible by water – the city as it was designed to be seen, through snatched glimpses into ancient houses, secluded gardens and boatyards with gondolas awaiting repair (*see page 79*).

4 Ecclesiastical Venice

The 200-plus churches of Venice boast some of the city's finest architecture, and many are also crammed with the most astonishing works of art too: **Madonna dell'Orto** (*see page 30*), the **Frari** (*see pages 56–7*), the **Scuola Grande di San Rocco** (*see pages 58–9*) and **La Salute** (*see page 78*), to name but a few.

5 The Canal Grande

The 'high street of Venice' is almost too good to be true. Sweeping graciously through the city, flanked by crumbling *palazzi* with their distinctive Venetian windows and their ground floors so frequently awash, and bustling with all manner of boats, this most beautiful of waterways is like a life-sized stage-set. Admire it from the front seats of a *vaporetto* (water-bus), and take plenty of film (*see pages 26–7, 41, 52, 73 and 92*).

6 The Lagoon

The outlying islands (*see pages 128–41*) offer a taste of Venetian life off the main tourist drag. From the glamorous, lively beach resort of the **Lido** to the glassworks of **Murano**, the multi-coloured houses of **Burano** and the outlying oasis of the nearly deserted **Torcello** – the choice is yours.

7 Night-time Venice

To capture the magical beauty of the floodlit main monuments, the deserted alleys and canals by night, stroll along the **Zattere** (the southern shore of Dorsoduro; *see page 79*), with its boathouses, bars and cafés, at dusk, when Venetians take their *passeggiata* (promenade). Indulge yourself in the romance of a twilight gondola ride, and end your day Venetian-style, with an ice-cream or a *digestif* in one of the many café-ringed squares.

8 Palazzo Ducale

Gleaming on the waterfront like a frosted pink birthday cake with lacy white icing, the Doge's Palace is undoubtedly the city's most magnificent *palazzo*, a veritable masterpiece of Gothic architecture. Inside, the dazzling treasures of the Republic provide a fascinating insight into Venice's colourful history (*see pages 96–9*).

9 Piazza San Marco

The heart of Venice for over a millennium, and celebrated by Napoleon as 'the most elegant drawing room in Europe', this square (*see page 100*) is where the city's heart beats loudest. Millions of visitors flock to see its magnificent buildings, for a mid-morning coffee on the most famous café terraces of the world, and the sensational views from the top of the **Campanile** (*see page 92*), which on a clear day extend beyond the lagoon to the snow-capped Dolomite mountains beyond.

10 The Rialto

Don't just visit the famed **Rialto Bridge** (*see page 53*), one of the classic picture-postcard sights of Venice. Take time also to visit the **Rialto markets** (*see page 54*) – ideally at the crack of dawn, before the crowds arrive – for a vivid insight into the hard-working life of everyday Venetians.

CANNAREGIO

Cannaregio

Characterised by broad beautiful canals, crumbling façades, faded palazzi, fine churches and ancient inns, this tranquil district provides a taste of the humble working city beneath the tourist tinsel.

BEST OF
Cannaregio

***Getting there:** By water-bus: There are two main waterways, the Grand Canal and the Canale di Cannaregio (Royal Canal). On the Grand Canal, vaporetto No 82 stops at Ferrovia and San Marcuola, while No 1 also stops at Ca' d'Oro. Circular routes 41/42 or 51/52 (both clockwise) from Ferrovia cut up the Canale di Cannaregio, with stops at Guglie and Tre Archi, then round the northern shoreline of Cannaregio.*

***By train:** Venice's main railway station (Stazione Ferrovia dello Stato Santa Lucia) brings you into the westernmost part of Cannaregio.*

① The Canal Grande

Catch vaporetto No 1 or 82 from Ferrovia and travel the length of the Grand Canal. Better still, indulge yourself in the romance of a gondola ride. As Thomas Mann wrote in *Death in Venice*: 'Is there anyone but must repress a secret thrill, on arriving in Venice for the first time – or returning thither after a long absence – and stepping into a Venetian gondola?'
Pages 26–7

② Northern Cannaregio

Head off the beaten track and explore the northernmost parts of the district – an unspoilt residential area, surprisingly devoid of tourists, with some of the widest and most beautiful canals in Venice, criss-crossed by bridges and alleyways. This is the more leisurely and workaday side of Venice, with local stores, workshops and bars, and clean washing strung up between the peeling façades of shuttered houses. You may even see local oarsmen practising their rowing technique on some of the quieter canals. **Page 126**

③ The Ghetto

Just off the Canale di Cannaregio lies the world's oldest ghetto, historically one of the city's most fascinating quarters, where all Jews were forcibly concentrated in the sixteenth century. Today, the peaceful tree-shaded *campo* with its ramshackle tower-block housing retains a distinctive appearance, without a church or *palazzo*, and with surprisingly few balconies. Nearby, you can still taste traditional Jewish cuisine, prepared according to ancient Venetian recipes. **Pages 28–9**

④ The Gesuiti, Madonna dell'Orto and Santa Maria dei Miracoli

Marvel at the architectural wonders of Cannaregio's churches, the exquisite marble-clad church of Santa Maria dei Miracoli, the opulent interior of the Gesuiti and the quarter's cultural highlight, the beautiful Gothic church of Madonna dell'Orto, parish church and last resting place of the great Venetian artist **Tintoretto**.
Pages 28 and 30–1

⑤ The islands

The *vaporetto* pier **Fondamente Nuove** is the starting point for excursions to the outlying islands of the lagoon, in particular **Murano**, **Burano**, **Torcello** and **San Michele** (*see pages 130–41*). Should you miss one of the frequent boats, you can always nip into a quayside café for some light refreshment. **Page 32**

Tip

Gondoliers usually take their passengers on one of several set routes around the city, simply because nobody asks them to do anything more adventurous. Venturing off the beaten track is no more expensive and guarantees you a chance to become gloriously enchanted by the secret canals of this watery labyrinth. So, take the plunge. Hop on a gondola and request a tour of hidden Venice.

Tourist information

There is a small tourist information office (Azienda di Promozione Turistica) just inside the Stazione Ferrovia dello Stato Santa Lucia (*tel: 041 5298727, fax: 041 719078; open: daily 0900–1900*).

Ca' d'Oro

Calle Ca' d'Oro. Tel: 041 5328790. Open: daily 0900–1330. ££.
Vaporetto: Ca' d'Oro.

'The Ca' d'Oro is like the smile of a woman', remarked André Suarès. 'Its face breathes happiness and serenity, and the Grand Canal reflects it.' Certainly Ca' d'Oro boasts the most beautiful façade of all Venetian palaces.

The former home of the **Contarinis**, the great family that gave the city eight doges, it was originally completely gilded – hence the name 'House of Gold' – but the gold has long since eroded, leaving a fanciful pink and white stone façade, carved into fragile, lacy Gothic patterns.

The building was restored in the early twentieth century by philanthropist **Baron Franchetti**, who furnished the interior with precious paintings, frescos and sculptures. But apart from **Titian**'s voluptuous *Venus* and **Mantegna**'s *St Sebastian*, the real reason to visit is to enjoy some of the finest views of the Grand Canal.

❝ *Palaces here and there, arising from the water, standing straight, reflected in the water … some dazzlingly white, sparkling as though made of salt, the others clothed in black velvet by the sea air.* ❞

Diego Valeri, *Guida sentimentale di Venezia*

Campo dei Mori

Vaporetto: *Madonna dell'Orto*.

Be one of the few tourists who visit this small square, because it is rich in history and legend. It takes its name from three stone statues which protrude from the buildings – the brothers Rioba, Sandi and Afani, who came to Venice from the Peloponnese (then called Morea, hence the name Mori) to escape civil war. On arrival in Venice in 1112, these three silk merchants acquired the nickname Mastelli, because they came laden with 'buckets' of riches. With these, they built Palazzo Mastelli (overlooking Rio Madonna dell'Orto), distinguished on the façade by a sculpture of a man and his laden camel.

Of the brothers, 'Signor Antonio Rioba' – the corner statue with a comical nose remodelled in metal – is particularly dear to Venetians. For centuries he was their equivalent of Rome's Pasquino, a 'talking statue' used by discontented citizens and local wits as a noticeboard for anti-establishment complaints, or as a pseudonym for published satires. A further statue, sporting a turban, can be seen just along Fondamenta dei Mori, beside the house (*No 3399*) where **Tintoretto** lived for 20 years until his death in 1594.

Canal Grande

*The Grand Canal has been described as 'the finest street in the world' – an extraordinary watery highway known affectionately as the Canalazzo ('Little Canal'), which winds proudly for nearly 4km (2¹/₂ miles) in an inverted 'S' shape, splitting the city into two unequal parts. For many it is their first impression of Venice – a fascinatingly beautiful sight, lined by **200 palaces** built between the twelfth and eighteenth centuries, which seem to rise directly out of the water, together with warehouses, markets and even a casino.*

Once the realm of grand galleys and trading vessels heading for the Rialto markets, today the canal is crowded with *vaporetti*, launches, working barges and gondolas – 'churned by propellers, turbulent as a great river' (Fernand Braudel, *Venise*). The best way to appreciate this remarkable canal is to join them. Jump in a gondola, or *vaporetto* No 1 or 82, grab a front seat, sit back and admire the works of art which line the banks.

Ferrovia Santa Lucia takes its name from the saint whose church had to be bulldozed to build this ugly railway station. The opulent baroque church alongside is known as the **Scalzi** after the supposedly 'shoeless' Carmelites who founded it. The **Ponte degli Scalzi** is one of only three bridges knotting the two halves of the city together.

Soon after, you meet the wide, navigable **Canale di Cannaregio** (the only waterway in Venice called a 'canal', apart from the Grand Canal), which, along with the *sestiere*, takes its name either from the thickets of canes which once grew here, or from its former name: Canal Regio ('Royal Canal').

Further along, the city's winter casino is housed in the early Renaissance **Palazzo Loredan-Vendramin-Calergi** – a most impressive palace, where composer Richard Wagner met his death in 1883.

Palazzo Barbarigo (opposite San Stae *vaporetto* pier) still retains traces of its sixteenth-century exterior frescos, once a common feature of canal-front mansions. The yellow-fronted **Palazzo Grissoni-Grimani** next door was originally adorned by **Tintoretto** frescos. Just before Ca' d'Oro landing-stage, the magnificent **Ca' d'Oro** is Venice's finest Gothic *palazzo* (*see page 24*), and the thirteenth-century **Ca' da Mosto** (two palaces along from Rio dei Santi Apostoli), one of the oldest. Just before the Rialto Bridge, the austere white **Fondeco dei Tedeschi** was a major foreign merchants' headquarters during the Republic.

> " *For this evening I have ordered the singing of the gondoliers ... the gondolier gives strength and energy to his song, so that it echoes in the distance and spreads over the surface of the water. Far away a companion replies with the next verse, then the first takes up the song again, as though the one were the echo of the other. The greater the distance between them, the more beautiful the song.* "
>
> **Johann Wolfgang von Goethe,** *Italian Journey,* **1816–29**

Getting there: From Ferrovia to the Rialto Bridge. Vaporetto: *1 or 82.*

Gesuiti

Campo dei Carmini. Tel: 041 5286579. Open: daily 1000–1200, 1700–1900.
Vaporetto: *Fondamente Nuove.*

The highly ornate church of Santa Maria Assunta dei Gesuiti has a history of controversy. The Jesuits' close ties with Rome provoked Venetian hostility, and for many years they were refused entry to the city. Eventually, in 1714, they were granted permission to build this church.

The grandiose exterior prepares visitors for the dazzling interior – a mass of green and white marble, carved around the pulpit like great folds of floral fabric, which prompted W D Howells to remark, 'The workmanship is marvellously skilful, and the material costly, but it only gives the church the effect of being draped in damask linen … it is indescribably tableclothy' (*Venetian Life*, 1866).

Ghetto Nuovo

Campo del Ghetto Nuovo.
Vaporetto: *Ponte delle Guglie.*

'*Li Giudei debbano tutti abitar unidi*' – with these words, in 1516, the Republican Senate of Venice confined all Jews to live on one small islet in Cannaregio, as part of a major anti-semitic campaign throughout northern Italy. The area was named after a former foundry, or *geto*, there, hence the origin of the word 'ghetto'.

The ghetto was enclosed by a high wall and gates, which were locked at nightfall, and its residents were obliged to wear distinctive clothing so their activities could be monitored. By the seventeenth century there were over 5 000 Jews living here. In order to accommodate

66 *Underneath Day's azure eyes*
Ocean's nursling,
Venice lies,
A peopled labyrinth of walls. **99**

Percy Bysshe Shelley,
Lines written amongst the
Euganean Hills, **1818**

everyone in such a small space, they built the houses up to eight storeys high – an incredible height at this time, making them the first high-rise buildings in Europe. The synagogues (five in total, and among the oldest in Europe) were placed on the top floors as this was the only space with nothing between them and the heavens.

Although the ghetto was eventually opened up in 1797 by **Napoleon**, it has remained a largely Jewish quarter with specialised shops and the city's only kosher restaurant, **Gam Gam** (*Sottoportico del Ghetto Vecchio; tel: 041 715284; £*). A small **Museo Comunità Ebraica** in the square (temporarily closed for restoration) traces the Jewish community's history to the present day with walking tours and visits to the synagogues.

Madonna dell'Orto

Campo della Madonna dell' Orto. Tel: 041 2750494. Open: Mon–Sat 1000–1700; Sun 1300–1700. £. Vaporetto: Madonna dell'Orto.

Madonna dell'Orto is an exceptionally fine Venetian Gothic church, with a noble brick façade and a graceful interior decorated with works by **Tintoretto**, who lived nearby. It was built in the late fourteenth century by the **Humiliati**, a religious order that was eventually terminated because it became too wealthy, worldly and impious.

The church is officially dedicated to St Christopher, the patron saint of ferrymen, whose statue stands above the main entrance. It was renamed the 'Madonna of the Orchard' (*orto*) after a hefty statue of a Madonna and child fell unexpectedly from heaven one day into a nearby orchard – coincidentally the orchard of a local sculptor! The statue is in the side chapel here, but it is the church's outstanding paintings that draw most visitors to these northern outskirts today.

The most magnificent are two huge Tintorettos beside the main altar – *The Last Judgement* (on the right) and *The Sacrifice of the Golden Calf* (on the left), both curved at the top like a Gothic arch – and *The Presentation of Mary at the Temple*, also by Tintoretto, over the doorway to the right. The artist's tomb – a simple, unadorned slab of marble – lies in the chapel to the right of the main altar. Note the photograph reproducing **Giovanni Bellini's** *Madonna and Child* (in the first chapel on the left). The original was stolen in 1993 and its

> " If the Earthly Paradise where Adam dwelt with Eve were like Venice, Eve would have had a difficult time tempting him away from it with a mere fig. "
>
> **Aretino**

frame hangs empty beside the photograph in the hope that it might eventually be returned.

The ground plan of the interior is unusual in that it has chapels on the left but only altars on the right, as the adjoining cloister here precluded building. To compensate, the painting over the first altar on the right portrays an open-air chapel. Look up also at the galleries towards the front of the church: the left-hand one is open while the other is simply painted on.

As you leave the church, pause to admire the **ornate Gothic façade**, beautifully decorated with white niches, statues, arches and floral patterns that stand out against the red brickwork. The square here still has the original herringbone paving and is today a popular football ground for local boys.

Santa Maria dei Miracoli

Campiello dei Miracoli. Tel: 041 2750462. Open: Mon–Sat 0900–1700; Sun 0900–1130, 1300–1700. £. Vaporetto: *Rialto*.

Santa Maria dei Miracoli is among the most charming churches of Venice. A masterpiece of the early Renaissance, this little church was built in the 1480s by **Pietro Lombardo**, and is distinguished by its architectural simplicity, its exquisite carvings and its revetment of coloured marble. Most people stumble across it almost by accident, squeezed as it is on to a tiny island which appears to be perfectly made for it, cut into a rough triangle by three gently flowing canals.

The church was built to provide protection for the early fifteenth-century *Madonna and Child* portrait (at the altar), said to have miraculous powers. The interior has an almost magical quality about it with its vaulted roof and starry dome, although not everyone would agree: John Ruskin, for instance, acknowledged it as 'the best possible example of a bad style'.

Cafés and restaurants

Antica Mola
Fondamenta degli Ormesini 2800. Tel: 041 717492. £. Closed: Wed. A friendly, family-run *trattoria* near the ghetto, serving classic local dishes at canalside tables and in a small shady garden.

Fiaschetteria Toscana
Salizzada San Giovanni Crisostomo 5719. Tel: 041 5285281. £££. Closed: Mon lunch and Tue. Booking essential. This intimate, candlelit restaurant is among Cannaregio's finest, with an impressive menu of traditional Venetian cuisine (try the mixed seafood platter – *frittura della Serenissima*) and an equally admirable wine list, boasting over 150 wines from all over Italy.

Osteria alla Frasca
Corte della Carità 5176. Tel: 041 5285433. £. Closed: Thur. Titian once kept his canvases in this country-style hostelry hidden in a tranquil residential corner of Cannaregio. The pretty vine-covered terrace provides a delightful setting to enjoy a plate of pasta or a selection of tasty *cicchetti* (tapas-style snacks).

Palazzina
Rio Terrà di S Leonardo 1509 (beside Ponte delle Guglie). Tel: 041 717725. ££. Closed: Wed. Once a popular bar where local shopkeepers met for an *ombra* (a small glass of wine) at lunchtimes. Now a highly regarded canalside restaurant with simple furnishings, a simple, daily changing menu and excellent pizzas.

Vini da Gigio
Fondamenta San Felice 3628a (off Strada Nova). Tel: 041 5285140. ££. Closed: Sun evening and Mon. Booking essential. Overlooking a small canal, this elegant restaurant serves such Venetian specialities as *sarde in saor* (sweet and sour sardines), liver and onions and *baccala mantecato* (dried salt cod in a cream sauce). The recipes are all taken from ancient cookbooks and the wine list is excellent, as the name suggests.

Algiubagiò
Fondamente Nuove 5039. Closed: Thur. Before boarding the ferry to Murano, Burano or Torcello, grab a quick coffee, a snack or a freshly squeezed juice at this cheerful café-bar, ideally situated beside the ferry stop.

Caffè Costarica
Rìo Terrà di S Leonardo 1563 (opposite Campo S Lunardo). Closed: Sun. One of Venice's oldest coffee houses – more a shop than a café – serving quick, stand-up espressos at the bar, and refreshing iced coffees (*frappé*) in hot weather.

Shopping

Bruscagrin Il Fornaio
Strada Nova 3845. This bakery offers an exceptional variety of bread and mouth-watering cakes. Try the *pan del Doge* (fruit bread).

Pastificio Artigiano
Strada Nova 4292. It's hard to beat the home-made pasta here, the gondola-shaped packet pasta or the unusually flavoured varieties (beetroot, curry, cocoa) which make fun presents.

Coin
Salizzada San Giovanni Crisostomo 5787. This department store, the elegant flagship branch of the popular Italian chain, is good for everyday fashion and accessories.

Mori & Bozzi
Strada Nova 3822a. A great address for affordable, trendy designer shoes.

Nightlife

Casanova Disco Café
Lista di Spagna 158a. Open: daily 2200–0400. Venice's newest disco plays salsa on Wednesdays, rock and wave on Thursdays, smash hits and golden oldies on Fridays, and house music on Saturdays.

Casino
Palazzo Vendramin-Calergi. Open: Oct–Mar, 1600–0230. Gamble the night away at the Grand Canal's glitzy casino. Dress smartly, and remember your passport.

Bacari

You'll find a profusion of bacari *(traditional Venetian bars) throughout the city – cheap, cheerful places to mingle with locals over an* ombra *and* cicchetti. *Cannaregio's best* bacari *include* Alla Bomba *(*Cannaregio 4297, off Strada Nova; tel: 041 2411146*),* Cantina Vecia Carbonera *(*Ponte Sant'Antonio 2329, near Via Vittorio Emanuele; tel: 041 710376*) with occasional live music and* Ca' d'Oro *(*Calle Ca' d'Oro 3912; tel: 041 5285324*), arguably the most romantic, atmospheric* bacaro *in town, with an excellent wine selection and certainly the best* polpete *(spicy meatballs).*

Venice in Peril

It's not all plain sailing in Venice. There are too many tourists and too much pollution, plus the ultimate fate of a city built on water: the relentless advance of the sea (see pages 108–9).

Subsidence

Building Venice was no easy feat. The 100-plus marshy islands on which the city stands provided a poor foundation. Closely packed pinewood piles (over 8m (26ft) long) were driven through the mud and embedded in the layer of compressed clay below to make a firm basis for the houses above. Lack of oxygen underwater and the passing of time has petrified the piles, but the stability of the fluvial plain cannot be guaranteed. As a result, many monuments are under constant threat of subsidence, and of 170 Venetian bell-towers, few remain perpendicular.

CANNAREGIO

Pollution

Venice's worst threat comes from the ugly factory complex at nearby **Marghera**, which mushroomed out of control during the post-war industrial boom, with the inevitable pollution and toxic fumes. Today, despite rigid controls, 50 tons of sulphur dioxide a year combine with the salt air of the lagoon to create a lethal cocktail which corrodes Venice's fragile buildings and statuary.

People

Henry James once pertinently remarked, 'There are some disagreeable things in Venice, but nothing so disagreeable as the visitors.' The city is not only threatened by the ever-increasing numbers of visitors, but also by the slow decrease in her population – a further consequence of Marghera's industrial boom that may ultimately reduce the city to little more than a museum-piece, 'somewhere between a freak and a fairytale' (Jan Morris, *Venice*). Apart from tourism, there is little reason for locals to remain in Venice. Homes are small and gloomy, and most require radical restoration. The average age of Venetians is 45, with few children and one-third of the population over 60. Its per capita income is the lowest in the Veneto, while prices are the highest in Italy.

The future

And the future? Nobody knows. Countless schemes are afoot to help preserve the city, but the mayor remains philosophical: 'If Venice has any vitality left, it will seize the moment. If it is dead in human terms, it will die.' We can only wait and hope.

Santa Croce

The true working atmosphere of ancient Venice prevails in Santa Croce, a peaceful sestiere off the main tourist beat, tucked within the upper loop of the Grand Canal. The eastern part of the district, in particular, is rich in history and tradition, embracing within its tightly packed maze of narrow streets, alleys and waterways several intriguing churches and some of the city's grandest palazzi.

SANTA CROCE

Santa Croce

Getting there: By car: Park in one of the massive multi-storey car parks at Piazzale Roma. From here it is a short walk to the heart of Santa Croce.

By train: Venice's railway station (Stazione Ferrovia dello Stato Santa Lucia) is situated just across the Grand Canal from Santa Croce. Gondolas ferry passengers across the canal from the landing stage marked *traghetto* outside the station. Alternatively, walk across the Ponte degli Scalzi, just a short walk along the canal (to the left as you leave the main entrance).

By water-bus: Vaporetto *No 1* has stops at Piazzale Roma, Riva de Biasio and San Stae, all within Santa Croce sestiere. Vaporetto *No 82* also stops at Piazzale Roma.

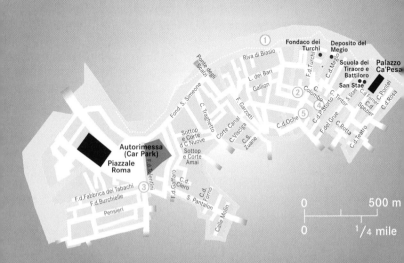

① *The Canal Grande*

Hop on a *vaporetto* (from **Piazzale Roma** landing-stage to **Ca' d'Oro**) to admire some of the finest *palazzi* of the Grand Canal. Remember to take plenty of film. **Pages 40–1**

② *San Giacomo dell'Orio*

Marvel at the mix of architectural and decorative styles, not to mention the ancient dignity, peace and sanctity, of San Giacomo dell'Orio, at the very heart of the *sestiere*. **Page 42**

③ *Tre Ponte*

Stand on the Tre Ponte (the curiously named 'Three Bridges', as there are actually *five* interlocking bridges here) and admire the extraordinary view of no fewer than twelve other bridges – a record in Venice. **Page 174**

④ *Ca' Mocenigo*

Still today, the sumptuous interior of Ca' Mocenigo, once owned by a wealthy dogal family, vividly illustrates the high standards of elegance that prevailed during the eighteenth century.
Page 40

⑤ *Pizzeria ae Oche*

The pizzas at Pizzeria ae Oche are reputedly the best in town. But allow plenty of time to choose, as the menu boasts over 90 varieties. **Page 44**

Tip

Be sure to take a detailed map when exploring Santa Croce. It is an undeniably labyrinthine quarter of sleepy, narrow streets, alleys and sottoporteghi *(covered passageways), with few signposts. If you do get irretrievably lost, follow signs to* **Piazzale Roma** *until you find yourself back on one of the main streets.*

Tourist information

There is no tourist information office in this district. The nearest one is at the railway station across the Grand Canal in Cannaregio (*see page 23*).

Ca' Mocenigo

Salizzada San Stae. Tel: 041 721789. Open: Mon–Sat 0830–1330 (library open Tue and Thur 0830–1330). ££. Vaporetto: San Stae.

Hidden down a back street near San Stae, this luxuriously furnished *palazzo* is a magnificent example of a seventeenth-century aristocratic residence. It is named after the great **Mocenigo family**, one of the city's oldest and wealthiest patrician families who over the centuries produced seven doges and purchased several splendid *palazzi* in Venice. Ca' Mocenigo began life as several neighbouring houses. The Mocenigo family converted it into a traditional *palazzo* towards the end of the sixteenth century, furnishing it with lavishly frescoed ceilings, Murano glass chandeliers and magnificent period furnishings. Alvise Mocenigo generously bequeathed this beautifully preserved *palazzo* to the city in 1954 (together with a small collection of fabrics and period costume) as a fascinating showcase of gracious patrician living. Step inside and experience the high life!

> " *Venice is not an expensive residence … I have my gondola and about fourteen servants … and I reside in one of the Mocenigo palaces on the Grand Canal.* "
>
> **Lord Byron in a letter to a friend, 1819**

Canal Grande

From Piazzale Roma to San Stae landing-stage. Vaporetto: *1 or 82.*

This stretch of the Grand Canal boasts a variety of notable palaces, including several Veneto-Byzantine architectural gems, and historic warehouses dating back to the times of the Serene Republic. Although heavily restored, it is easy to visualise them as they were, when they imported rice, spices, perfumes and dried fruits from the East.

After the **Ponte degli Scalzi** (one of just three bridges spanning the canal; *see page 27*) and the **Riva di Biasio** quayside (by the *vaporetto* stop, named after the butcher with a shop here, who was beheaded in 1520 for selling human flesh), the first warehouse of note (opposite San Marcuola landing-stage) is the impressive Veneto-Byzantine-style **Fondaco dei Turchi** ('Turk's Warehouse'), one of the largest buildings on the canal with a sumptuous marble arcaded façade. Originally built in 1250 as a private home, from 1621 to 1838 it was one of the city's greatest warehouses, rented to Turkish merchants as the headquarters of the Ottoman trade delegation in Venice. At the same time it served as a mosque, a bath-house and a bazaar. Later, as trade with the East began to decline, the palace was abandoned and fell into ruin. It was unsympathetically restored in the nineteenth century, and today houses Venice's **Museum of Natural History** (currently closed for long-term restoration).

Beside the Turk's Warehouse, but separated by Rio del Megio, the plain-brick **Deposito del Megio** ('Millet Deposit') served as the Republic's public granary, permanently stocked for times of war and famine. Look closely and you will see a relief of the Lion of St Mark (a modern replacement of one destroyed at the downfall of the Republic).

Further along the canal, the façade of **San Stae** (by San Stae *vaporetto* pier; *see page 43*) overshadows the shabby, red, faded **Scuola dei Tiraoro e Battiloro**, one of the smallest, most charming buildings on the Grand Canal. Once the headquarters of the goldsmiths' guild, it is now occasionally used for exhibitions. Two palaces down from San Stae, the Grand Canal affords an impressive view of **Palazzo Ca' Pesaro** (*see page 42*) with its white-marble, geometrically patterned façade.

Ca' Pesaro

Fondamenta Ca' Pesaro. Tel: 041 721127. Open: Tue–Fri 0900–1400; Sat and Sun 0900–1300 (last tickets 30 minutes before closing; ring the bell to get in). ££. Vaporetto: San Stae.

This grand palace is one of the great masterpieces of Venetian baroque, designed in the mid-seventeenth century by master architect **Baldassare Longhena**. The **curving marble façade** is especially remarkable, and is noted for its grotesque carvings of masks and monsters, and its sculptural use of light and shade.

> " Palaces here and there, arising from the water, standing straight, reflected in the water, in two parallel, continuous rows, following the slow curve of that blue 'S' … some dazzlingly white, sparkling as though made of salt, the others clothed in black velvet by the sea air. "
>
> **Diego Valeri, *Guida sentimentale di Venezia***

Unbelievably, the *palazzo* has been undergoing restoration since 1981. At present only the top floor is open, where you will find the **Museo Orientale**, a hotchpotch of Asian artefacts including some notable Japanese paintings, armour, lacquer-work and bronzes – worth a visit, if only for the canal views. The **Museo d'Arte Moderna**, noted for its comprehensive collection of nineteenth- and twentieth-century art (also in the *palazzo*), is currently closed.

San Giacomo dell'Orio

Campo San Giacomo dell'Orio (entrance in Campiello del Piovan). Open: Mon–Sat 1000–1700; Sun 1300–1700. £. Vaporetto: Riva di Biasio.

San Giacomo dell'Orio is one of the city's most ornate churches. Built during the ninth and tenth centuries, it has been the focal point of Santa Croce for centuries. From the exterior, it is difficult to see how the church is oriented, with its clumsy, bulbous apses and stocky thirteenth-century *campanile* ('bell-tower'). As with many older Venetian churches, the main entrance faces the canal rather than the main square.

Once inside, you will be struck by its initial resemblance to **Basilica San Marco**, albeit on a smaller scale. But look closer and you will discover a fascinating mix of architectural and decorative styles, with ancient Byzantine capitals (including one made of green *verde antico* marble), wooden Gothic arches and plump Renaissance apses all crowned by a magnificent fourteenth-century wooden ship's-keel roof, built to limit the church's weight on the once swampy ground.

The origin of the name 'Orio' is unknown, but it is believed to come either from *luprio* ('marshy land') or *lauro*, after the laurel trees in the picturesque square that surrounds the church.

Not only does the church have great intrinsic charm, it also contains some fine artwork, including five paintings by **Veronese** on the new sacristy ceiling, **Lotto**'s late *Madonna and Four Saints* in the presbytery and, on the pier to the left of the main altar, an unusual sculpture of the Virgin waving.

San Stae

Campo San Stae. Tel: 041 2750462. Open: Mon–Sat 1000–1730; Sun 1500–1730. Vaporetto: *San Stae.*

The seventeenth-century church of Sant' Eustachio ('San Stae' in Venetian dialect) has a dramatic late-baroque façade. Essentially Palladian in form, its four pillars are crowned by a triangular tympanum, and it is embellished by a number of spirited saint sculptures.

The bright, newly restored interior is a temple to eighteenth-century art, notably (in the lower left row) the *Martyrdom of St James the Great* by **Piazzetta** and *St Peter Freed from Prison* by **Sebastiano Ricci**, and, opposite, **Giambattista Tiepolo**'s *Martyrdom of St Bartholomew*. A slab in the floor, with the Latin epitaph 'Name and ashes buried together with vanity', marks the grave of **Doge Alvise Mocenigo II**, who financed the stately façade.

Cafés and restaurants

Antica Bessetta
Salizzada de Ca' Zusto 1395. Tel: 041 721687. £££. Closed: Tue, and Wed lunch. Booking advisable. Intimate, family-run restaurant offering authentic Venetian cuisine at its best, washed down with the family's own wines. Specialities include *risi e bisi* (spring pea risotto) and *grancevola* (spider crab from the lagoon).

Brodo di Giuggiole
Fondamenta Minotto 158. Tel: 041 5242486. ££. Closed: Mon. This smart new restaurant, alongside a canal near Piazzale Roma, really comes into its own in summer, with its cool, shaded garden and excellent fish menu. But save room for the delectable *tiramisu del Doge*!

Al Ponte
Calle Larga (beside Ponte Megio) 1666. Tel: 041 719777. £. Closed: Sat evening and Sun. A typically Venetian locale, serving classic *trattoria* fare at canalside tables. Try the hearty bean soup for starters, followed by *fritto misto* (seafood fry-up).

La Zucca
Calle del Megio 1762. Tel: 041 5241570. ££. Closed: Sun. Booking advisable. This tiny, modern restaurant overlooking the canal offers an inventive menu of home-made pasta dishes, vegetarian specialities and seasonal salads.

Al Vecio Fritoin
Calle della Regina 2262. Tel: 041 5222881. £. Closed: Mon, and Tue lunch. One of the last *fritoin* in Venice, maintaining the ancient tradition of *fritto en scartoso* (crispy fried fish to take away, wrapped in paper and served with *polenta*). For those wishing to sit down, there is a full *trattoria* menu too.

Pizza

*Santa Croce is blessed with more than its fair share of top pizzerias. Al Nono Risorto (*Sottoportico de Siora Bettina; tel: 041 5241169; £; closed Wed*) gets the student vote for the best pizzas in town. Da Crecola (*Campiello del Piovan; tel: 041 5241496; ££*) has the prettiest setting, with outdoor tables in a delightful canalside campiello beside San Giacomo dell'Orio. Ae Oche (*Calle del Tintor; tel: 041 5241161; £*), with 90-plus varieties, has the largest selection, while Al Gallo (*Corte Amai; tel: 041 5205953; ££; closed Sat*) has some of the most unusual toppings, including spiced pizza with marjoram, sesame seed, poppy seed, mint, thyme, fennel, basil and juniper.*

Shopping

Arca
Calle del Tintor 1811. Tiny shop bursting with brightly coloured, modern, chunky ceramics. The hand-painted vases, tiles, plates and pendants, in particular, make fun gifts.

Boutique del Dolce – Gilda Vio
Fondamenta Rio Marin 890. Reputedly the best patisserie in Venice. The unforgettable *tiramisu* is a must for anyone with a sweet tooth.

Toni dalla Venezia
Calle Pesara 2074. Toni still uses the traditional Venetian technique of *tira-ora* (gold-leaf decoration) to make exquisite gilded wooden frames in his atmospheric studio.

Guido Farinati
Calle Larga 1658 (off Campo San Giacomo dell'Orio). Examples of Farinati stained glass can be seen throughout Venice – in the Doge's Palace and Torcello cathedral, for instance. Guido Farinati continues the age-old family tradition, producing fine pieces of mosaic-style stained-glass, and other quality glass giftware.

Nightlife

Ai Postali
Fondamenta Rio Marin 821. A favourite haunt of students, either for early-evening aperitifs or late-night drinking with background jazz. In summer there's a terrace beside the canal.

Alla Rivetta
Calle Sechera. A tiny bar, popular for a glass of *prosecco* and some top-notch *cicchetti* (*see pages 170–3*).

Old Well Pub
Corte Canal 656. Just off Piazzale Roma, this pub serves an excellent pint and is always lively.

Carnival

Close your eyes and imagine an enchanted evening during carnival: a tall man in a dark cloak and a tricorn hat sweeps past, whispering 'Benvenuto al carnevale', and disappears into the mist-wrapped streets; your gondola arrives and glides through the inky waters to a magnificent candlelit palace on the Grand Canal where you dance until dawn in a whirl of plumes, sequins and masqueraded revellers ...

As if Venice did not have enough visual attractions, the city is transformed every year (in the days leading up to Lent) into a spectacular pageant of wonderful costumes and elaborately decorated masks, of parties, parades, open-air concerts and, most lavish of all, the Doges' Ball.

Carnival celebrations began in Venice more than a thousand years ago when the period leading up to Lent became a time of excessive and wild partying. The wearing of masks began

SANTA CROCE

as a tradition to enable nobles to mix incognito with ordinary folk: men dressed up as women, masters as servants, servants as masters; a masked aristocratic lady could act out her fantasies, making love to a gondolier without him knowing her true identity. The whole city went berserk! By 1458, the revelry had become so licentious that an edict was issued preventing men from entering convents in women's clothing to commit *multas inhonestates*!

By 1790, carnival in Venice had grown so popular that it lasted from November until March. Many Venetians wore their masks throughout, and party-goers would travel across Europe to join in with the debauchery and thrill of the celebrations. However, party-pooper Napoleon put a stop to it all in 1797, outlawing the carnival. The tradition was not renewed again until as recently as 1979.

Today, Venice's world-famous carnival is a much tamer affair. Visitors are encouraged to take part and can buy a disguise from any number of street stalls and shops – anything from a traditional Commedia dell' Arte character to the most extravagant and bizarre costumes. The merry-making lasts for ten days, ending with the tolling of the bells of San Francesco della Vigna at midnight on Shrove Tuesday, but not before a massive firework display over the lagoon rounds off the celebrations in spectacular style.

San Polo

For centuries, lively San Polo, the smallest and most ancient sestiere, has been the hub of commercial Venice, with its narrow alleys and tiny campielli and its familiar landmark, the Rialto Bridge.

BEST OF
San Polo

Getting there: On foot: *Throughout Venice, you will find bold yellow signposts indicating 'Rialto'. From Santa Croce and Dorsoduro, these will lead you straight to the busty Rialto district of San Polo beside the Grand Canal. Likewise, from Cannaregio, San Marco and Castello, follow the signposts to Rialto, then cross the bridge into San Polo.*

By water-bus: *To reach San Polo by* vaporetto, *hop aboard either No 1 or 82 (both of which ply the Grand Canal), disembarking at Rialto. Remember that the landing-stages are on the San Marco side, in Riva del Ferro. Simply cross the bridge to San Polo.*

By gondola: *Shortly before the end of the Riva del Vin quay, a gondola shuttle service connects San Polo with Riva del Carbon in the* sestiere *of San Marco on the opposite side of the Grand Canal.*

① The Rialto

Explore the Rialto district – a maze of dark, narrow streets brimming with cafés, hidden squares and appealing market stalls. The tastes, fragrances and colours of the fruit and vegetable market in particular are a feast for the senses. **Page 54**

② Rialto shopping

For centuries, this district was the commercial centre of Venice, and still today the streets retain their ancient names: Casaria ('cheese-makers'), Saoneri ('soap-makers'), Botteri ('barrel-makers'), Speziali ('spices'), Cappeller ('milliners') and Cordaria ('rope-makers'). The streets from the Rialto to Campo San Polo are lined with tempting boutiques and, what's more, prices here are generally cheaper than in San Marco. **Page 61**

③ Scuola Grande di San Rocco

Visit this remarkable place, undoubtedly one of the great sights of Italy, housing the largest collection of works by **Tintoretto** in Venice, if not worldwide. **Pages 58–9**

④ Rialto churches

Take refuge from the midday heat in one of San Polo's countless churches – in tiny **San Giacomo di Rialto**, for instance, reputedly the oldest church in Venice, or in the vast Gothic **Santa Maria Gloriosa dei Frari**, the city's largest and most important church after Basilica San Marco. **Pages 55 and 56**

⑤ The Rialto Bridge

Get a bird's-eye view of the Grand Canal from atop the Rialto Bridge, one of the city's most famous landmarks and for centuries the only bridge that spanned the canal. **Page 53**

⑥ The Canal Grande

Gliding down the Grand Canal by gondola at twilight with a loved one by your side may well be a cliché, but it promises to be one of the most unforgettable moments of your visit. Start at the gondola jetties below the bridge, and head north, turning left into the quiet backwaters of San Polo and Santa Croce. **Page 52**

Tip

For a glimpse of everyday Venetian life, get to the Rialto markets early and watch the local shop-keepers, farmers and fishermen who meet every morning before the sun rises to unload their boats along the quaysides of the Grand Canal, and set up their stalls ready for the day's trade.

Tourist information

There is no tourist information office in this district. The nearest ones are either near St Mark's Square (Calle Larga dell'Ascensione; *see page 87*) or at the railway station across the Grand Canal in Cannaregio (*see page 23*).

Canal Grande

From San Stae to San Tomà landing-stage. Vaporetto: *1 or 82.*

For centuries, the busy area around the Rialto Bridge has been a centre of trade. Today, crowded quaysides, ancient administrative buildings and colourful food markets still border this stretch of the canal.

The **Fondamenta dell'Ogio** quayside takes its name from the olive oil that was once unloaded here. Today it is chock-a-block with colourful barges and fishing boats. Just beyond, there has been a thriving fish market at **Campo di Pescaria** for six centuries; today it takes place under the white arches of a mock-Gothic market hall (by the Santa Sofia *traghetto* stop). The following ungainly pink and white market buildings, the **Fabbriche Vecchie** and the **Fabbriche Nuove**, were built in the sixteenth century as offices of the judiciary for trade and commerce. Just before the **Rialto Bridge**, the elegant white sixteenth-century **Palazzo dei Camerlenghi**, cornering the canal, was originally the city treasury, with a debtors' prison on the ground floor.

After the bridge, the **Riva del Vin** quayside is one of the few places where you can sit and relax at a waterside table on the banks of the Grand Canal. At the end of the quay, the Gothic **Palazzo Donà** is often referred to as *alla Madonnetta*, after the early Renaissance Madonna set into its façade. Further down, past several undistinguished *palazzi* and beside the broad entrance to Rio di San Polo, **Palazzo Ca' Barbarigo della Terrazza** takes its name from the magnificent rooftop terrace overlooking the canal.

> " *I will buy with you, sell with you, talk with you, walk with you, and so following: but I will not eat with you, drink with you, nor pray with you. What news on the Rialto?* "
>
> **Shylock, in William Shakespeare's**
> ***The Merchant of Venice**, I.iii.30–4*

Finally, just before San Tomà landing-stage (on the corner of Rio di San Tomà), you will find the faded yellow **Palazzo Marcello 'dei Leoni'**, named after the venerable stone lions guarding the doorway.

Ponte Rialto

Vaporetto: *Rialto*.

It is said that the very first inhabitants of Venice settled here on a cluster of small islands called Rivus Altus ('high bank') or Rialto, the height of the land affording them greater safety from flooding than the surrounding islands. By the eleventh century, Rialto had become the commercial centre of an ever-expanding city.

Today, the familiar Rialto Bridge, which spans the Grand Canal like a giant frowning eyebrow, is the last in a long line of bridges linking San Polo with San Marco. The first – a simple wooden pontoon bridge – appeared around 1172, and was called 'Quartarolo' after the coin paid to cross it; the second disappeared during a revolt in 1310; and the third collapsed under a wedding procession in 1444. An artist's impression of its successor (complete with drawbridge and shops) can be seen in **Carpaccio's** painting *The Miracle of the True Cross at the Rialto Bridge* in the **Accademia** (*see pages 68–71*).

In the sixteenth century, it was decided to replace the wooden bridge with a sturdy marble structure. A competition was held and many architects submitted plans, including **Michelangelo**, **Palladio**, **Sansovino** and **Da Ponte**, whose design was chosen (perhaps because of his name?). Begun in 1588, the daring single-arched bridge with a span of 28m (92ft), and lined with a double row of shops, took just three years to complete, despite the site's instability (the foundations required over 12,000 piles) and the added difficulty of making it high enough to enable state galleys to pass beneath. Until 1854, when the Accademia Bridge was constructed, the Rialto Bridge remained the only means of crossing the canal on foot.

Rialto markets

Erberia: Mon–Sat until noon; Pescheria: Tue–Sat until noon. Vaporetto: *Rialto.*

Few sights in Venice are as colourful and animated as the Rialto markets, with their appealing blend of noisy, gesticulating locals, traders and tourists. For centuries this was the centre of business and trade – here you could buy everything from gold, silver and oriental silks and spices to fish, fruit and vegetables – and the surrounding streets developed into a maze of shops, taverns and offices, set up by the Republic to manage the increasingly sophisticated maritime trade of the city.

It is still easy to imagine the Rialto markets as they were in their heyday. Stroll through the streets and squares near the Rialto Bridge – along the **Erberia** quayside (fruit and vegetable market) and through the porticos of the **Pescheria** (fish market) with its glistening fresh fish – and absorb the 'ancient smell of mud, incense, fish, age, filth and velvet' (Jan Morris, *Venice*). It may no longer be the centre of Venetian trade, but it is still undoubtedly the most buzzing and picturesque part of town for shopping.

> " *If Saint Mark's Square is the royal throne room; the Quay the splendid balcony overlooking the lagoon; the grand canal the gallery of pictures and mirrors; Rialto is what might be called the city's larder …*"
>
> **Diego Valeri, *Guida sentimentale di Venezia***

Riva del Vin

Vaporetto: *Rialto.*

The Riva del Vin, where wine was once off-loaded from boats, is one of only a few accessible quaysides along the Grand Canal. Beside the Rialto Bridge and a mere stone's throw from the local markets, it is a surprisingly tranquil spot to enjoy a drink or a meal, or merely to watch the comings and goings of traffic on the canal.

San Giacomo di Rialto

Campo San Giacomo. Open: daily 1030–1200, 1600–1730 (except Sun afternoon). Vaporetto: *Rialto*.

Tradition has it that the church of San Giacomo at Rialto is the oldest church in Venice, dating back to the fifth century. Even though this is not strictly true (the current building dates from the twelfth century), the Venetians are still particularly fond of their little church, which catches the eye of so few tourists. Indeed, they often refer to it in the diminutive form – **San Giacometto** – not only because it is small, but also as a term of endearment.

Before entering the church, take time to study its unique exterior: the **lean-to portico**, of a type once common in Venice, but now one of just two surviving examples, and, its most eccentric feature, a **huge 24-hour clock** whose face, since its installation in the fourteenth century, has more often than not shown the wrong time. At times its hands have been stuck in the same place for so long that art historians have been able to date paintings by it.

The Veneto-Byzantine interior of the church follows the Greek cross plan of the first church, decorated with ancient Greek columns. During the Middle Ages, the church was home to a number of guilds related to commercial activities in the area. The goldsmiths, exchange merchants and cheese-sellers had altars here, as did many other merchants.

On leaving, note outside (on the apse) the medieval injunction aimed at the market stall-holders: 'Around this Temple, Let the Merchant's Law Be Just, His Weights True, and His Promises Faithful'.

In the square outside, the sixteenth-century statue known as the **Gobbo** ('hunchback') **di Rialto**, bent double under the weight of the stairs above, is an allegory of the heavy taxes heaped on Venetians over the centuries. Criminals used to be condemned to run all the way from Piazza San Marco to this statue, while jeering onlookers hurled abuse and dealt them blows.

Santa Maria Gloriosa dei Frari

Campo dei Frari. Open: Mon–Sat 0900–1800; Sun 1500–1800. £. Vaporetto: San Tomà.

After St Mark's Basilica, Santa Maria Gloriosa is Venice's next largest and most important church. It was built in 1250 by the Franciscans, hence its popular name, I Frari ('the friars'). Although the exterior is unprepossessing, the vast Gothic interior shelters some of Venice's most dazzling art treasures.

The most famous of these is **Titian's** *Assumption* (1518) over the main altar, one of the most influential paintings in sixteenth-century Venetian art. It portrays the ascension of the Virgin, in robes of brilliant 'Titian red', to heaven on a cloud supported by floating cherubs. When the friar who commissioned the painting first saw it, he didn't want it, because it was so different from the accepted style of the time. Mary appeared as a real woman of flesh and blood and not as she was usually represented – as a being of unearthly beauty. The painting is best viewed from the back of the church, where it appears 'framed' by the marble rood screen.

Titian's second major work, *Madonna di Ca' Pesaro* (1526), though not as powerful as the Assumption, nevertheless reflects his mastery of light and colour. Other noteworthy works of art include a triptych, the *Madonna Enthroned with Saints* (1488), painted on wood by Bellini, and a primitive wooden sculpture, *St John the Baptist* (*c* 1450), by **Donatello**.

Because the friars were held in such high esteem, the Frari was considered a most prestigious place of worship. As a result, a number of important Venetians are buried here, including **Doge Pesaro** and **Doge Tron**, marked by two huge and lavish funerary monuments. By contrast, the composer **Monteverdi** is remembered by a simple, unadorned white marble slab on the floor. The pupils of sculptor **Canova** created a peculiar pyramidal tomb for him and a vast neo-classical monument to Titian, which probably makes him turn in his grave.

> " *The tomb of Canova cannot be missed; consummate in science, intolerable in affectation, ridiculous in conception, null and void to the uttermost in invention and feeling.* "
>
> **John Ruskin, *Works***

San Polo

Campo di San Polo (entrance in Salizzada San Polo). Open: Mon–Sat 1000–1700; Sun 1300–1700. £. Vaporetto: San Tomà.

The ancient church of San Polo gives its name to the *sestiere*. The building is an unusual combination of architectural styles, as a result of numerous alterations since its foundation in the ninth century and a major restoration in 1804, which proved so expensive the church was forced to sell some of its finest treasures.

Unless you are interested in **Tintoretto**'s dramatically realist *Last Supper*, or **Tiepolo**'s stunning cycle the *Via Crucis* (seventeen small canvases representing stations of the cross), stay outside and devote your attention to the striking brick façade. The entrance has a Gothic portal made of different coloured marble, and at the base of the bell-tower, on the opposite side of the street, there are two carved lions: one clasps a serpent in its claws, the other the head of **Doge Falier**, who was punished for treason.

Beyond the church, **Campo di San Polo**, the largest square in Venice after St Mark's, was once the scene of bullfights, mass sermons, street parties and masked balls. Today it remains one of the main carnival venues, and is also used for open-air concerts and screenings during the film festival. Pause awhile at one of its small cafés to admire the various handsome façades, and the **fountain** – a rare sight in Venice.

Scuola Grande di San Rocco

The Scuola Grande di San Rocco is the most magnificent of the Venetian scuole *(charitable lay confraternities) and one of the greatest city sights. Its remarkable collection of epic canvases by Tintoretto led John Ruskin to describe it as 'one of the three most precious buildings in Italy' (alongside Rome's Sistine Chapel and Campo Santo at Pisa).*

Its name originates from the Greek *scuole*, or 'association for the purposes of prayer, edification and mutual assistance'. These associations began to flourish throughout Europe in the Middle Ages, supported by various guilds, and fulfilled a religious purpose as well as helping their members: the sick and the needy. Thanks to generous donations over the centuries, their buildings reached great heights of splendour, and their members played a leading role in the economic life of the city.

> *We shall scarcely find four walls elsewhere that enclosed within a like area an equal quantity of genius … It is not immortality that we breathe at the Scuola di San Rocco, but conscious, reluctant mortality.*
>
> **Henry James, *Venice*, 1882**

The Scuola Grande di San Rocco was established in 1478 as a place for worship and to care for the sick following the 1477 plague. It was dedicated to **St Roc**, the protector of plague victims. The building we see today was constructed between 1489 and 1549, its two floors reflecting the transition from Renaissance to baroque. Visitors were received on the ground floor, while the upper floor was reserved for confraternity meetings.

Once the building was completed, the Scuola launched a competition to find a painter to decorate the rooms. Each participant had to submit a sketch of St Roc ascending into heaven. Jacopo Tintoretto, already a famous artist, craftily deceived everyone by hanging a finished painting behind a curtain where the winning picture was to be hung. He even gave the painting to the school as a present. Needless to say, he won the competition, and over the next 25 years he proceeded to adorn the walls with a staggering 54 masterpieces, giving this commission priority over all other work assigned to him in Venice.

To view Tintoretto's works in chronological order, start in the Great Hall on the first floor, where you will find on the ceiling his **21 Old Testament scenes**, and on the walls **10 New Testament episodes**, the most famous being those devoted to the life of Christ. Many, such as *Christ Heals the Paralytic* and *The Multiplication of Bread and Fishes*, reflect the brotherhood's purpose of assisting the sick and needy.

The last canvases Tintoretto painted for the Scuola are on the ground floor. These focus on **key episodes in the life of Mary** (*The Flight into Egypt, Mary of Egypt, The Assumption*), while his largest, and perhaps greatest, masterpiece, **The Crucifixion**, hangs upstairs in the Albergo Hall. It is particularly remarkable for its rapid brushwork, its sculptural rendering of the figures and for the marked contrasts of light and shade, with the light around Christ representing the triumph of good over the forces of darkness and the hope of resurrection. The oval painting on the ceiling here is said to be the 'sketch' that won Tintoretto the Scuola's commission.

Getting there: Campo San Rocco. Tel: 041 5234864. Open: daily 1000–1600. £££ (includes 45-minute audio-guide). Vaporetto: San Tomà.

Bars and restaurants

There are plenty of eateries to choose from in San Polo, especially around the Rialto markets. Should you tire of Italian cuisine, why not try Venice's only Indian restaurant, **Ganesh Ji** (Calle de l'Orio; tel: 041 791804; ££; closed Wed) *or the tiny, top-notch Chinese,* **La Perla d'Oriente** (Campo dei Frari 3004; tel: 041 5237229; ££)?

Cantina Do Spade
Calle Do Spade 860. Tel: 041 5210574. £. Closed: Thur lunch and Sun. Hidden down a dark alley near the Rialto, this cosy *osteria* with its simple home cooking was a favourite haunt of the great Venetian lover **Casanova**.

Da Fiore
Calle dello Scalater 2202a. Tel: 041 721308. £££. Closed: Sun and Mon. Booking essential. A veritable temple of Venetian *alta cucina* (*haute cuisine*), with discrete décor and service, fine local wines and an exceptional selection of regional cheeses and desserts.

Da Ignazio
Calle dei Saoneri 2749. Tel: 041 5234852. ££. Closed: Sat. A long-established *trattoria* with a courtyard garden, known for its traditional seafood dishes, served with a twist. Try the baby octopus in balsamic vinegar, or poached spider crab and nettle pie.

Do Mori
Calle dei Do Mori 429. Tel: 041 5225401. £. Closed: Wed lunch and Sun. The oldest *bacaro* (traditional bar) in Venice, a stone's throw from the Rialto, and a lively place to try the local wines and a snack. The *tramezzini* (tiny filled sandwiches) are especially recommended.

Poste Vecie
Pescaria 1608. Tel: 041 721822. £££. Closed: Tue. One of Venice's best fish restaurants, in a cosy, wood-panelled, ancient posthouse opposite the Rialto fish markets. Specials depend on the day's catch.

San Tomà
Campo San Tomà 2864a. Tel: 041 5238819. ££. Closed: Tue. This popular *trattoria* serves delicious pizzas and pasta dishes outside in the pretty piazza or, at the height of summer, in the cool garden within its walls.

Shopping

Bambolandia
Calle Madonnetta 1462. Open: Mon–Thur morning; Fri and Sat all day. A genuinely old-fashioned toy shop, with rocking horses, dolls, teddies, books … even Pinocchio.

Colorcasa
San Polo 1990. Full to the brim with cushions, curtains, tapestries, tassels and other sumptuous Venetian textiles.

Emilio Ceccato
Sottoportici Rialto 16–17. The place to buy a genuine gondolier shirt or stripy top.

Gilberto Penzo
Calle II dei Saoneri 2681. A boat-lover's delight, this tiny workshop sells kits of over 70 different models, from historic gondolas to classic yachts.

Legatoria Polliero
Campo dei Frari 2995. The diaries, notebooks and photograph albums of this traditional bookbinder make exquisite gifts.

Valeria Bellinaso
Campo Sant' Aponal 1226. Beautiful hats, scarves and handbags by local Vicenza-born designer Valeria Bellinaso, in richly coloured silks and luxuriant velvets.

Nightlife

The Scuola di San Giovanni Evangelista (*Campiello de la Scuol; tel: 041 5228125*) and the Scuola Grande di San Rocco (*see page 58*) provide magnificent settings for classical music concerts, featuring the music of Gabrieli, Cavalli, Monteverdi and other composers from the Veneto school, whose names have long been associated with these prestigious venues. Some concerts are performed in period costume and on original instruments.

Picnic fare

This is the *district to stock up for a picnic. Buy salad and fruit at the Rialto market stalls (* Mon–Sat mornings *); bruschette and herb-flavoured* grissini *from the bakery Mauro (* Ruga Rialto 603 *); regional cheeses (* montasio, piave, asiao *) from Latteria Ronchi Francesco (* Ruga Rialto 1053a *); and wine, cold cuts, olives and sun-dried tomatoes at Aliani (* Ruga Rialto 654 *), the best delicatessen in town.*

Death in Venice

There is something undeniably haunting and melancholic about the crumbling majesty of Venice 'sitting among her stagnant lagoons, forlorn and beggared' (Mark Twain, The Innocents Abroad*), with its palaces 'like grey symbols of the grave' (Jan Morris,* Venice*) and its gondolas 'black as nothing else on earth except a coffin' (Thomas Mann,* Death in Venice*).*

Venetian history has long been an arena for death and drama, an atmospheric backdrop for untimely ends both in fact and fiction, a figment of the romantic imagination fired by such literary classics as Thomas Mann's classic *Death in Venice* (made into a film by Visconti in 1971) and numerous modern murder mysteries. Even politician Enric Miralles remarked in 1999, 'I am sure Venice can come to no decision without referring to its ghosts.'

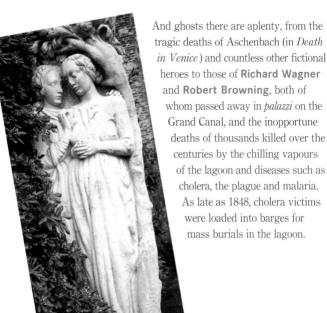

And ghosts there are aplenty, from the tragic deaths of Aschenbach (in *Death in Venice*) and countless other fictional heroes to those of **Richard Wagner** and **Robert Browning**, both of whom passed away in *palazzi* on the Grand Canal, and the inopportune deaths of thousands killed over the centuries by the chilling vapours of the lagoon and diseases such as cholera, the plague and malaria. As late as 1848, cholera victims were loaded into barges for mass burials in the lagoon.

Today's main cemetery, on the island of San Michele, contains the graves of such celebrities as **Diaghilev**, **Stravinsky** and **Ezra Pound**, all of whom breathed their last in Venice (*see page 137*). Nowadays the cemetery is full, and to make space for new arrivals coffins are dug up after ten years and the bones placed in a public ossuary, unless there is enough money to lease a family plot. Gondola hearses are easily identifiable – they are royal blue – and funeral cortèges a particularly moving sight: 'the death-boat chugs away through the mist down the Grand Canal, with a glimpse of flowers and a little train of mourning gondolas' (Jan Morris, *Venice*).

Today, the city continues its close ties with death in its astonishingly high suicide rate – not among natives, but visiting foreigners. A leading psychiatrist suggests they see Venice as 'a beautiful, unreal city at the end of the line. The dark mixture of death and water provides a deadly, irresistible allure.'

Dorsoduro

No one should miss this atmospheric neighbourhood with its tightly knit tangle of picturesque canals, quiet calle *and tiny, sun-bleached squares.*

Getting there: By water-bus: Vaporetto No 1 on the Grand Canal stops at San Tomà, Ca' Rezzonico, Accademia and Salute. Nos 51 and 52 stop at Zattere. **By gondola:** To cross from San Marco to Dorsoduro by gondola, look out for the following traghetto landing-stages: from Sant' Angelo to San Tomà; from San Samuele to Ca' Rezzonico; from Santa Maria del Giglio to the vicinity of Collezione Guggenheim; and from Piazza San Marco to Salute.

On foot: All the places described here are easily accessible by foot. From neighbouring districts, follow the large yellow signposts indicating Accademia.

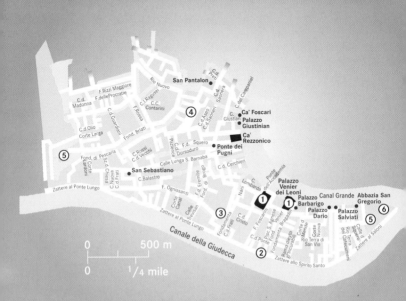

① The Accademia and the Collezione Guggenheim

Visit these two top-notch galleries on the banks of the Grand Canal, the former the world's greatest collection of Venetian paintings, and the latter a must for fans of contemporary art – and, after the Accademia, the second most visited museum in Venice.
Pages 68–71 and 74–5

② The Zattere

The mile-long Zattere, which forms the sweeping southern quayside of Dorsoduro, is one of the liveliest promenades in the neighbourhood, and a great place to dally over a coffee or lunch on one of several sunny café terraces overlooking the Giudecca Canal, followed by a delicious ice-cream for dessert at **Da Nico**, reputedly the best *gelateria* in town. **Page 79**

③ Squero di San Trovaso

It is fascinating to watch the skilled workers building and repairing their shiny black gondolas at Squero di San Trovaso, one of the very few traditional boat-building yards still in operation.
Page 79

④ Campo Santa Margherita

Pause awhile in Campo Santa Margherita to take in the everyday atmosphere of this spacious square with its popular cafés and market stalls, and its constant bustle of chattering locals, hurrying students and pottering pigeons. **Page 72**

⑤ Dorsoduro churches

This historic part of Venice contains numerous ancient churches, from the humble **San Nicolò dei Mendicoli**, one of the city's oldest churches, hidden in a little-known former fishermen's quarter, to the colossal majesty of **Santa Maria della Salute**, the pinnacle of the baroque movement in Venice. Despite some dreary façades, you will find that inside they are all sparkling oases of history and art.
Pages 76–8

⑥ Dogana di Mare

Stroll through the picture-postcard backstreets of Dorsoduro, through a district that once seduced such artists as **Canaletto**, **Turner**, **Monet** and many others. End your walk outside the Dogana di Mare just in time to see the setting sun silhouetting **Palladio's great church of the Redentore** on the distant island of Giudecca. **Page 75**

Tip

As Dorsoduro is the major district for art lovers, choose which day you visit with care. On Mondays the Accademia shuts in the afternoon; on Tuesdays the Collezione Guggenheim is closed; and on Fridays it is the turn of Ca' Rezzonico. The best days to visit, therefore, are Wednesdays, Thursdays or Saturdays. Then again, you could always just wait for a rainy day.

Tourist information

There is no tourist information office in this district. The closest one is near St Mark's Square at Calle Larga dell'Ascensione (*see page 87*).

Accademia I

Not only is the Accademia the city's most popular gallery, it is also the world's finest collection of Venetian art, including masterworks from its most famous sons, from **Giorgione** *and* **Veronese** *to* **Titian**, **Tiepolo** *and* **Tintoretto**.

The collections are housed in **La Carità**, a complex of church, convent, cloisters and *scuole*. The church was deconsecrated in Napoleonic times, and used as a repository for the art treasures of the Venetian Republic saved from the many monasteries and churches Napoleon closed down. But the main nucleus of the new Accademia di Belle Arti (Academy of Fine Arts), as it became known, came from a pre-existing collection – the Accademia dei Pittori e Scultori – which had been assembled by the Venetian artists of the eighteenth century.

The main entrance is in the former Scuola Grande di Santa Maria della Carità – the side entrance is reserved for art students attending the adjoining art school. There are polyglot descriptive cards available in most of the **24 rooms**, but the collection is a little confusing as it is not always in chronological order. The first 11 rooms focus on the Renaissance, while rooms 12 to 17 display eighteenth-century landscapes and genre paintings, before reverting to the Renaissance for the remaining rooms.

" *There are surely in Venice more paintings than in all the rest of Italy.* **"**

– written in a 1561 guidebook to Venice

Room 1 of the collection was originally the meeting room of the Scuola, the oldest of the six Scuole Grande of Venice. The ceiling is the work of **Marco Cozzi** from Vicenza, a brother of the confraternity – note the witty series of eight-winged angel heads, each portrayed with a different expression. The *pièce de resistance* of the fourteenth- and fifteenth-century artworks here is **Veneziano**'s polyptych, *The Coronation of the Virgin*, which bridges the gap between Byzantine art and the beginning of a truly Venetian school of painting, with its tentative three-dimensionality and characterisation in the side panels.

Room 2 was constructed to house Titian's *Assumption*, which has since returned to its native church, the **Frari** (*see pages 56–7*). Today, in its place are several fine Renaissance altarpieces, including **Giovanni Bellini**'s beautiful *Madonna and Child Enthroned*, originally in San Giobbe, which drew such admiration from its contemporaries that it served as a model for several later altarpieces. Beside it, on the left, **Carpaccio**'s *Presentation of Jesus at the Temple* was also originally in San Giobbe. It is especially striking for its vivid colours, the beautiful faces of the women and the fine attention to detail, down to the minute scenes from Genesis and the Apocalypse decorating the robes of Simeon, the high priest.

You'll find the next major highlights in Room 5. Many consider Giovanni Bellini's *Pietà* (1505) his absolute masterpiece, while the quirky *Madonna degli Alberetti* ('of the trees') of 1487 is the first dated work (beneath the Child's feet) by the artist – a powerful image enhanced by the luminous, narrow strips of landscape on either side.

Getting there: Campo della Carità 1050. Tel: 041 5200345. Open: summer, Mon 0900–1400, Tue–Fri 0900–2100, Sat 0900–2300, Sun 0900–2000; winter, Mon 0900–1400, Tue–Sat 0900–1900, Sun 0900–2000. Guided tours: Wed and Thur 1000, 1100, 1200 (in English); Fri 1030, 1130, 1230 (French); Tue–Sun 1000, 1100, 1200 (Italian). £££. Vaporetto: *Accademia.*

Accademia II

Also in Room 5, *The Tempest* by Giorgione is one of the landmarks in the history of Western art, the very first painting in which landscape and the changing moods of nature were attributed so much importance. Furthermore, by abandoning any formal compositional arrangement or preparatory drawing, and by freely building up the image through layers of superimposed paint, he laid the foundations for modern painting. Special radiography has revealed a seated nude woman painted under the soldier on the left and several similar figures embedded in the layers of paintwork.

The moving *Young Man in his Study* in Room 7 is one of Lotto's most famous portraits, the rose petals, ring, letters and a tiny lizard on the table all alluding to the frailty of life, and possibly a lost or unrequited love.

By contrast, the huge, lively Veronese canvas in Room 10, *The Feast at the House of Levi*, was originally a Last Supper commissioned for the monastery of Santi Giovanni e Paolo, to replace the *Last Supper* by Titian, which was destroyed by fire. However, its light-hearted, profane mood so outraged the Church that Veronese was given three months to correct it. Unable to oblige, Veronese simply renamed it. Also in Room 10 you will find a celebrated *Pietà* by Titian and several Tintorettos, including the powerful *Dream of St Mark*, dazzling in its use of light and shade.

" *How does one recognise Venetian paint? By a brilliance of colour, some say ... by a greater luminosity, say others ... By the subject matter, many would confess, meaning the milky-breasted goddesses of Titian, Tintoretto and Veronese, or the views of Guardi and Canaletto. I would say it identifies itself ... by an enhanced reality, a reverence for the concrete world.* "

Mary McCarthy, *Venice Observed*, 1961

A little further on, there is a corridor of delightful seventeenth- and eighteenth-century Venetian landscapes and a series of genre paintings in the small rooms alongside. There are surprisingly few works by Canaletto in Venice (partly due to his long stay in England), but you will find three in Room 17, together with six enchanting vignettes by Pietro Longhi, gently satirising everyday scenes of Venetian nobility. The attention to detail is so minute that the painting within *The Pharmacy* can be identified as a work by **Antonio Balestra**, still in a private Venetian collection.

In the last few rooms, we return to the Renaissance on a grand scale, both in quality and size. Highlights include **Gentile Bellini's** *Procession* in Room 20 – a valuable insight into St Mark's Square with its rose-coloured brick paving, the ancient bell-tower and the basilica agleam with its original mosaics. Opposite, **Carpaccio's** *Miracle of the True Cross at the Rialto Bridge* shows the ancient wooden bridge, together with traditional gondolas steered by gondoliers in splendid costumes. Room 21 contains Carpaccio's fabulous cycle *The Legend of Saint Ursula* – one of *the* artistic sights of Venice – nine brilliant canvases famed for their evocative scenes, fine attention to detail and frequent allusion to Venice.

Finally, Room 24 (the **Sala dell'Albergo**, where meetings of the Scuola were held) preserves its original panelling, its fifteenth-century ceiling with the four evangelists and Titian's *Presentation of the Virgin*, actually painted for this room – the perfectly balanced composition of architecture, landscape and procession led, of course, by the confraternity.

DORSODURO

Ca' Rezzonico
(Museo del Settecento Veneziano)

Fondamenta Rezzonico 3136. Tel: 041 2410100. Open: Oct–Mar, 1000–1600; Apr–Sept, 1000–1700; closed Fri. ££. Vaporetto: *Ca' Rezzonico.*

Not only is this one of the few *palazzi* on the Grand Canal which opens its doors to the public, but it also happens to be one of the finest – an outstanding example of baroque architecture designed by the prestigious Venetian architect **Baldassare Longhena**. The **Rezzonico family** moved here in 1687. They were neither Venetian nor aristocrats, but they were rich and important enough to buy themselves noble rank from the Republic.

Today, the newly restored palace houses the **Museum of Eighteenth-century Venice**. Within its sumptuous rooms you will find an enormous ballroom lavishly decorated with *trompe-l'œil* frescos, various **Guardi**, **Canaletto** and **Tiepolo** artworks, some exotic chinoiserie, an unusual nuptial chamber with two dressing-rooms, and an entire pharmacy reassembled from Campo San Stin. With so many original furnishings and paintings still in pristine condition, it is easy to conjure up a vivid picture of patrician life in eighteenth-century Venice.

Campo Santa Margherita

Vaporetto: *Ca' Rezzonico.*

This large, lively square is where Dorsoduro's heart beats loudest. Unlike the tranquil surrounding canals and *calle*, Campo Santa Margherita vibrates with life throughout the day. In the morning, a small market provides the focal point; in the afternoon it belongs to children, and old folk who watch the world go by from the shaded terraces of restaurants and cafés; by night, the bars of the Campo attract a young, trendy crowd.

Alone in the middle of the square, the **Scuola de Varoteri** (Tanners' Guild) once overlooked a canal. On its wall is a plaque specifying the minimum lengths acceptable for the fish sold at market here.

Canal Grande

From vaporetto *stops San Tomà to Salute.*

Dorsoduro's span of the Grand Canal has more than its fair share of patrician palaces, especially after the *volta* ('curve'), when the canal becomes wider and grander than ever. The magnificent Ca' Foscari (beside Rio di Ca' Foscari), built for Doge Foscari in 1437, is now part of Venice University. Composer Richard Wagner lived next door at Palazzo Giustinian from 1858 to 1859, and wrote the second act of *Tristan und Isolde* here. Ca' Rezzonico (just before Ca' Rezzonico landing-stage), with its imposing pillared façade, was once the home of English poets Elizabeth Barrett and Robert Browning. It now contains the Museum of Eighteenth-century Venice.

" *Obviously things have to smell of whatever they smell of, and obviously canals will reek in the summertime, but this really is too much.* **"**

Burgundian president Charles de Brosses, eighteenth century

After Accademia Bridge, Palazzo Barbarigo (on the corner beside Rio San Vio) stands out as a result of its harsh mosaics, added in 1887. Alongside, the single-storey Palazzo Venier dei Leoni is a more unusual landmark – a truncated, white, unfinished palace housing the Guggenheim Collection of modern art.

Two palaces further on, and lavishly decorated with coloured marble, is the higgledy-piggledy Palazzo Dario (marked 'Darius' on the façade), said to bring bad luck to its owners, all of whom have died in a mysterious or violent way. The most recent was industrialist Raul Gardini, who shot himself in 1992 rather than face charges of corruption. Nearby, Palazzo Salviati (opposite Santa Maria del Giglio landing-stage), decorated with garish modern glass mosaics, was built by one of Murano's glass barons.

Just before Santa Maria della Salute, the tiny brick church of Abbazia San Gregorio is all that remains of a once powerful monastic centre. Today, it is used as a laboratory for the restoration of large-scale paintings. The Grand Canal ends with a flourish at the monumental La Salute and the Dogana di Mare (Maritime Customs), both with sweeping views across the water towards St Mark's Square.

Collezione Guggenheim

Palazzo Venier dei Leoni. Tel: 041 5206288. Open: Wed–Mon 1100–1800, with presentations in English at 1200 and 1600. ££. The museum is in the process of acquiring the Dogana di Mare as further exhibition space for those works currently in storage. Vaporetto: Accademia.

The Guggenheim Collection counts among the most important contemporary art museums in the world. Housed in the quirky Palazzo Venier dei Leoni on the Grand Canal, this unfinished single-storey white *palazzo*, aptly nicknamed 'Palazzo Nonfinito', has long attracted eccentric characters.

In the eighteenth century the **Vernier family** kept a pet lion chained in the garden, hence the 'dei Leoni'. In the early twentieth century the flamboyant socialite Marchesa Casati of Milan sprayed the grounds lilac and filled them with apes, Afghan hounds and naked, torch-bearing 'slaves' for one of her notorious parties. In 1949, the palace was purchased by American copper heiress **Peggy Guggenheim**, who lived here until her death in 1979. An ardent collector, dealer and patron of modern art, over the years she built up a remarkable collection of over 200 paintings and sculptures. On her death, the building and the collection were given to the Guggenheim Foundation created by her uncle, Solomon R Guggenheim.

Of the open-air sculptures dotted about the gardens, be sure to see **Giacometti**'s *Donna 'Leoni'*, **Brancusi**'s *Bird in Space* and **Marini**'s startling *Angel of the Citadel* – an equestrian astride his horse, erect in every respect, and provocatively placed facing the Grand Canal for all passing *vaporetti* to see.

Inside the *palazzo*, the collection is exceptional for its range, quality and comprehensiveness, representing all the major twentieth-century art movements, especially the Surrealists. The list of artists is truly impressive,

and includes **Bacon**, **Braque**, **Chagall**, **Kandinski**, **Klee**, **Magritte**, **Mondrian** and **Moore**. One entire room is dedicated to Peggy's own discovery, **Jackson Pollock**; the dining room contains **major Cubist works**, including **Picasso's** *The Poet*; there is even a room devoted to her daughter Pegeen (a talented primitive painter who committed suicide at the age of 45), and several works by Peggy's second husband, **Max Ernst**, including *The Kiss* and a curiously grotesque *Robing of the Bride*.

The museum is sure to thrill those who appreciate modern art. Those who do not will enjoy the gardens (where Peggy is buried with her 14 poodles), the café, the gift shop and the view of the Grand Canal.

Dogana di Mare

Punta di Dogana. Closed to the public. Vaporetto: *Salute.*

The ancient Maritime Customs House boasts some of the finest views in Venice from its location at the easternmost point of Dorsoduro, overlooking St Mark's Basin and the islands of **San Giorgio** and **Giudecca**. Strolling along the quayside and under the arches of this historic building, it is easy to imagine the sailors of bygone days tying up their vessels alongside to pay duty on goods arriving from the overseas dominions of La Serenissima. For a long time, the salt supplies of the Republic were kept in storerooms here. On the top of the Customs House, a gleaming golden globe is supported by two bronze figures of Atlas, and crowned by a weathervane – appropriately enough, the goddess of Fortune.

> " *The statue of Fortune, in the form of a weathervane standing atop the world, gives a true idea of the perceptions of the time, and of the hopes and ideals of the last great days of Venice.* "
>
> **John Ruskin**

Ponte dei Pugni

Fondamenta Gherardini (Rio San Barnaba). Vaporetto: *Ca' Rezzonico.*

" *The palaces and churches, in their great masses, rise light and miraculous like the harmonious dream creations of some young god.* "

Ivan Turgenev

Unlike most of Venice's 400-plus bridges, the Ponte dei Pugni ('Bridge of Fists') once played a key role in city life. For centuries, the citizens of Venice were divided into two opposing factions: the **Castellani** (from Castello, San Marco and Dorsoduro) and the **Nicolotti** (from Cannaregio, San Polo, Santa Croce and the San Nicolò parish of Dorsoduro). The bridge marked the border between them, so they would meet here periodically for official 'punch-ups' – vicious fights involving hundreds of men trying to throw as many of their foes as possible off the bridge into the water. These battles lasted several hours, with many deaths. They were eventually prohibited in 1705, but the white marble footprints on the bridge still denote the starting points for each fight. Thankfully, today, the only crowds here are the locals shopping at the **San Barnaba Barge**, the most photogenic greengrocer's in town, moored alongside the bridge.

San Nicolò dei Mendicoli

Campo San Nicolò. Tel: 041 5285952. Open: daily 1000–1200, 1600–1800. Vaporetto: *San Basilio.*

Hidden away from tourist areas in a peaceful, tree-shaded square flanked by canals and brightly coloured fishing boats, the simple church of San Nicolò exudes peace, dignity and holiness. This part of eastern Dorsoduro was one of the earliest areas to be settled in the lagoon, by poor folk, fishermen, sailors and salt-pan workers, hence the name San Nicolò 'dei Mendicoli' ('of the beggars').

A church stood here as early as the seventh century, but today's building, with its Veneto-Byzantine layout and mullioned windows, dates from the Middle Ages. The leaning loggia at the entrance served as a shelter for the homeless. The interior contains a delightful hotchpotch of artwork, including some beautiful gilded wooden statues and a series of paintings on the life of Christ by **Alvise dal Friso** and other pupils of Veronese.

San Pantalon

Campo San Pantalon. Open: Sun–Fri 1600–1800. Vaporetto: *San Tomà.*

San Pantalon is among the most visually striking churches in Venice – don't be put off by the lacklustre, unfinished façade! Once inside, you will be overwhelmed by the epic ceiling painting – **The Martyrdom and Glory of St Pantalon** – by the little-known seventeenth-century artist **Fumiani**. A veritable *tour de force* of *trompe-l'œil* and perspective, it was created on sixty panels before being hoisted into place, making it the largest area of painted canvas in the world. It took Fumiani 24 years to complete this breathtaking ceiling. Ironically, while stepping back to admire the finished work, he fell from the scaffolding to his death, and was humbly buried in the church under a seat.

San Sebastiano

Campo San Sebastiano. Open: daily 1000–1700. £. The sacristy and choir are currently closed for restoration. Vaporetto: *San Basilio.*

An early sixteenth-century church, often praised for being a perfect marriage of art and architecture. This is largely owing to the artist **Veronese**, the last great painter of the Venetian Renaissance and a master of spatial illusion in decorative art, who from 1555 to 1565 smothered the lofty interior (even the organ shutters) with lavish frescos.

Although he was not a native of the city, Veronese's exuberant work, with its rich colours and sumptuous costumes, embodied the spirit of La Serenissima at the height of its power. These brilliant paintings, depicting the Virgin Mary (in the sacristy), Esther (on the ceiling of the nave) and San Sebastian (on the side walls of the chancel) count among his finest works. It seems only fitting that he is buried in the church.

Santa Maria della Salute

Campo della Salute. Tel: 041 5225558. Open: daily 0900–1200, 1500–1730.
Vaporetto: *Salute.*

Described by art critic Bernard Berenson as 'the building which occupies the centre of the picture Venice leaves in the mind', this **magnificent baroque church** of monumental proportions is undoubtedly one of the great architectural sights of Venice – a shining white riot of domes and statues, supported by over a million timber piles and guarding the entrance to the Grand Canal. It was built to commemorate the end of the 1630 plague, which had wiped out over one third of the population (hence the name 'Salute', meaning health and salvation).

Its designer, **Baldassare Longhena**, worked on the church for half a century, dying five years before it was completed. The end result, consecrated in 1672, counts among Venice's most spectacular churches, with its octagonal basilica encircled by chapels and surmounted by a great cupola, conceived as a 'crown for the Virgin Mary, the protector of the city', to whom the church is dedicated.

The massive main entrance is only opened on 21 November, the feast day of Madonna della Salute, a key date in the Venetian calendar, when a bridge of boats is constructed across the Grand Canal, enabling people to walk across the water to worship. The interior hinges on the contrast between the light of the central section and the semi-darkness of the circular aisle.

" *The classic Salute waits like some great lady on the threshold of her salon … with her domes and scrolls, her scalloped buttresses forming a pompous crown and her wide steps disposed on the ground like the train of a robe.* "

Henry James, *The Grand Canal*, 1892

Stand in the centre of the church. It is the only spot from which you can see all the altars simultaneously. The best paintings are in the sacristy, and include three allegorical paintings on the ceiling by **Titian**, and **Tintoretto's** *Marriage in Cana* to the left of the altar.

Squero di San Trovaso

*Campo San Trovaso/
Rio di San Trovaso.
Closed to the public.*
Vaporetto: *Zattere.*

Of Venice's few
remaining gondola
workshops, this is
the oldest, and the
only one where
gondolas are still
made according to ancient tradition, with timber from
the Cadore area of the Dolomites. It was founded in the
seventeenth century by a family from the mountains, hence
the Tyrolean look of the surrounding buildings. Although
the workshop is closed to the public, you can usually see
workmen repairing upturned gondolas from the far side of Rio
San Trovaso. You may even be lucky enough to see a new
one, although nowadays they make only about ten a year.

Zattere

Vaporetto: *San Basilio or Zattere.*

This long promenade bordering the Giudecca Canal is a great
Venetian favourite, stretching from the Customs House to
the maritime station. It takes its name from the large wooden
rafts (*zattere*) used for unloading cargo, which once lined the
waterfront. In 1519 they were replaced with an
elegant stone quay, but the name remained.

The original rows of warehouses remain,
including the ancient s*alone* (salt warehouses).
Throughout the Middle Ages, the city held the
salt monopoly for the region. It was the only
raw material produced locally, and a major
source of income. Most warehouses have since
been converted into restaurants, rowing clubs
and artists' studios. The liveliest stretch is
around **Gesuati church** and the boat-stops to
the Giudecca. On a sunny day, it is a wonderful
spot to sit at a waterside café, watching the
world go by.

Bars, cafés and restaurants

Ai Gondolieri
Fondamenta di San Vio 366. Tel: 041 5286396. £££. Open: daily 1200–1445, 1900–2200. Closed: Tue. Booking advisable. Unusual in Venice – a fish-free restaurant. This genuine old inn is renowned for its exceptional meat and vegetable dishes from the Veneto, including such delicacies as *risotto al radicchio* (chicory) and duck seasoned with butter and sage.

L'Incontro
Rio Terra Canal 3062. Tel: 041 5222404. ££. Open: Tue–Sun 1230–1430, 1930–2230. Closed: Mon. Booking advisable. A tiny rustic restaurant with a Sardinian chef, Sardinian specialities and Sardinian wines. Try the exceptional *tagliata di manzo* (finely sliced steak with lemon and rosemary). In mild weather there is a small pavement terrace.

Al Profeta
Calle Lunga San Barnaba 2671. Tel: 041 5237466. ££. Open: daily 1200–1430, 1900–2230. Closed: Mon. This cheerful, popular restaurant serves delectable pizzas and a conventional *trattoria* menu in its pretty, sheltered garden.

Da Toni
Fondamenta San Basilio 1642. Tel: 041 5286899. £. Open: Tue–Sun 0600–2000. No credit cards. A no-frills local *osteria* with simple home cooking and tables outside along a pretty canal opposite San Sebastiano.

Il Caffè
Campo Santa Margherita 2963. Open: Mon–Sat 0740–0200. Pause awhile and watch the Venetian world go by from the terrace of this tiny café, nicknamed 'Caffè Rosso' after its distinguishable red awnings.

Cantina del Vino già Schiavi
Fondamenta Meravegie 992. Open: Mon–Sat 0900–1300, 1515–2030. A friendly bar within a fine old wine shop, run by three generations of the same family. Standing room only. In summer, everyone spills out on to the picturesque canal quayside.

Margaret DuChamp
Campo Santa Margherita 3019. Open: daily 0800–0200. This sophisticated café is currently one of *the* places to see and to be seen in.

Da Nico
Zattere ai Gesuati 922. Open: daily 0700–2200. The speciality of this ice-cream temple on the Zattere, reputedly the best in town, is *giandiotto*: praline ice-cream with lashings of whipped cream.

Shopping

Dorsoduro is a fantastic district for traditional crafts. At lace specialist **Annelie** (*Calle Lunga San Barnaba 2748*) you'll find a beautiful selection of clothing and table linens. **Camilla** (*Campo dei Carmini 2609*) creates imaginative pottery dishes, vases, buttons and ornaments inspired by the Venetian landscape, and at **Cornici Trevisanello** (*San Vio 662*), picture frames are still made using traditional techniques of gilding and glass inlay. **Il Grifone** (*Fondamenta del Gaffaro 3516*) produces smart, simple leatherware – everything from belts and wallets to filofaxes and rucksacks – and **Il Pavone** (*Fondamenta Venier dei Leoni 721*) sells exquisite hand-blocked marbled paper. The **Sent-Sanvio** showroom (*Campo San Vio 669*) displays modern designer jewellery and glassware made by sisters Marina and Susanna Sent, and **Mondonovo** (*Rio Terra Canal 3063*) is indisputably the best mask shop in town.

Coffee

Coffee is an essential part of Venetian life. Indeed, the beverage was first introduced to Europe as a medicinal drink by traders of the Serenissima in the early seventeenth century. Venice's first coffee house opened in 1683 in St Mark's Square, and started the Italian fashion for coffee-drinking. Italians rarely drink coffee with milk, favouring espresso, *a tiny, extra-strong coffee prepared expressly for you (hence the name) and drunk piping hot early in the morning (to wake them up), after meals (helpful to digestion) and during the afternoon (as a break from work). For a less concentrated coffee, ask for a* caffè lungo. *For coffee with milk, choose* caffè con latte, caffè macchiato *(with just a dash of milk) or* cappuccino *(served in a large cup with hot frothy milk and a sprinkling of cocoa powder).*

Nightlife

Dorsoduro is one of the liveliest *sestieri* for nightlife, with plenty of late-night bars and cafés. The most popular include **Il Caffè** and **Margaret DuChamp** (*see above*) in Campo Santa Margherita, and the student haunts **Café Blue Pub** and neighbouring **Café Black** (an internet café by day and a popular bar by night), both in Calle dei Preti Crosera and open until 0200.

For live music, **Café Blue** has the occasional rock band. For jazz on Tuesday nights, try the laid-back, arty wine bar **Da Codroma** (*Fondamenta Briati 2540; open: Fri–Wed 1900–0200*). For something more smoochy and upmarket, there's the chic Linea d'Ombra restaurant-cum-piano bar on the **Zattere** (*Zattere Ai Salone 19; open: 2000–0200, except Wed and Sun*), with its sensational cocktails and romantic waterside views.

There's even a disco in Dorsoduro: **Il Piccolo Mondo** (*Calle Contarini Corfu 1056a; open: Thur–Tue 2200–0400*), playing commercial house music for a young, gay-friendly crowd.

Painting Venice

Few cities can equal Venice's artistic riches, considering the lavish adornment of its churches, its palazzi and its public buildings. Centuries of trade with the East left a bold imprint on the city's 1 000-year art history, with the shimmering Byzantine-influenced icons and mosaics of St Mark's Basilica and Torcello providing inspiration for generations of painters, attracted by their vibrant colours, luminosity and decorative detail – hallmarks of Venetian art.

Because of its passion for Byzantium, Venice was slow to adopt the Renaissance. Giovanni Bellini was the city's first true Renaissance painter. His radiant altarpieces (in the Frari, San Zaccaria, the Accademia and elsewhere) count among the city's most sublime artworks. His brother, Gentile, was better known for his *istorie* (history paintings), with which he decorated the Doge's Palace.

During the sixteenth century, Venetian art thrived with such homegrown talent as Titian and Tintoretto. Titian, known for his

virtuoso style and brilliant use of colour (Titian 'red'), is badly represented in Venice, apart from certain masterpieces in the Frari (*see pages 56–7*) and the Accademia. By contrast, few painters have left their mark on Venice so firmly as his rival, Tintoretto, the son of a local dyer (hence his name, meaning 'Little Dyer'). His canvases – astonishing for their scale, complexity and deft brushwork – grace numerous buildings throughout the city, including the **Madonna dell'Orto** (*see pages 30–1*) and the **Scuola Grande di San Rocco** (*see pages 58–9*).

After Titian and Tintoretto, artistic supremacy shifted to **Rome**, home of the baroque. But Venice re-emerged during the eighteenth century with the advent of colourful, lavish masterworks by **Tiepolo**, the greatest painter of the Venetian rococo, while Antonio Canal (better known as **Canaletto**) crafted his magnificent Venetian *vedute* (landscapes).

By the Napoleonic conquest in 1797, the capital of the artistic world had shifted to Paris. Venetian art, rather like its military power, was a spent force. Ever since, the city has been a honey-pot for foreign artists, and with the **Collezione Guggenheim** and the **Biennale** it is nowadays an important venue for the exhibition of contemporary art.

SAN MARCO

San Marco

For centuries San Marco has been the true heart of Venice. Visitors and locals alike are drawn, as if by magnet, to the crowded St Mark's Square to marvel at such 'must-sees' as the Basilica and the Doge's Palace.

Getting there: By gondola: If you are in Dorsoduro and want to treat yourself to a gondola ride, look out for traghetto landing-stages at San Tomà, Ca' Rezzonico, Collezione Guggenheim and Salute.

By water-bus: Vaporetto No 1 on the Grand Canal stops at Rialto, Sant' Angelo, San Samuele, Giglio and San Marco. Vaporetto No 82 and the night boats (marked N) stop only at Rialto, San Samuele and San Marco.

On foot: Three main thoroughfares link the key points of San Marco, forming a rough triangle. One leads from Piazza San Marco to the Rialto, another runs from Piazza San Marco to the Ponte dell'Accademia, and the third links the Rialto and the Ponte dell'Accademia. All are clearly indicated with large yellow signposts.

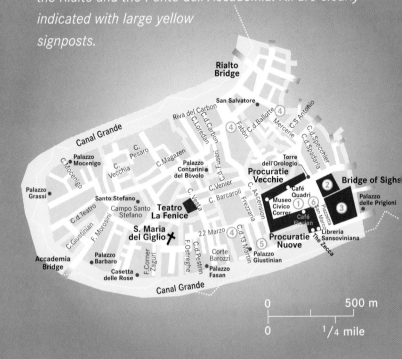

① Piazza San Marco

It is easy to spend a full day at St Mark's Square. So many of the city's major sights are here or nearby. It is also a wonderful place to stroll, to relish the café orchestras, to window-shop and to feed the pigeons. And be sure to have coffee in **Quadri** or **Florian**. The price will take your breath away, but so too will the atmosphere and the views.
Pages 100–3

② Basilica San Marco

The Basilica of San Marco is one of the greatest churches in the world, and the spiritual heart of ancient Venice. Visit during mass to see the 4 000 square metres of mosaics within its gleaming golden interior magically illuminated, and be sure to walk out on to the loggia for an unusual view of St Mark's Square. **Pages 88–91**

③ The Doge's Palace

The grandest of all the *palazzi* and Venice's former political centre, the palace stands as an astonishing legacy of the city's heyday as a world capital and mighty sea power under the medieval leadership of the doges. Step inside and wind the clocks back to the glorious days of La Serenissima.
Pages 96–9

Tourist information

Venice's main tourist office (Azienda di Promozione Turistica) is just off St Mark's Square, never more than a few minutes' walk from all the sights in this area (*Calle Larga dell'Ascensione 71; tel: 041 5298711, fax: 041 5230399, website: www.provincia.venezia.it/aptve, email: aptve@provincia.venezia.it*).

④ San Marco's shops

It is hard to resist the beautifully dressed shop windows that line the *sestiere*'s busy, narrow streets. The **Mercerie**, stretching from the Rialto to St Mark's Square, has been Venice's main shopping street since the Middle Ages, while Via XXII Marzo, Calle dei Fabbri and the streets around St Mark's Square boast glitzy big-name designer boutiques and smart speciality stores.
Page 107

⑤ Harry's Bar

Top your day off with a sensational Bellini cocktail at the most celebrated bar in Venice, particularly famed as a favourite of Ernest Hemingway.
Page 106

⑥ The Campanile

For a pigeon's-eye view of St Mark's Square and the entire city laid out at your feet, go up the Campanile. There is a lift to whisk you to the top, where it is fun to spend half an hour picking out your hotel, your favourite canal, the gleaming cupolas of churches and other city landmarks. **Page 92**

Tip

Please note that shorts, bare arms and shoulders, and skirts above the knee are prohibited for men and women entering St Mark's Basilica. Should you not adhere to this strict dress code, you will be turned away at the door. In addition, photography is forbidden, and you must remain silent at all times.

Basilica San Marco I

The Basilica of St Mark is, without doubt, Venice's most famous building – a 'church of gold' which has maintained an aura of mystery over the years that both tourists and Venetians find captivating. The biggest mystery surrounds its construction: to this day, no one knows who was responsible for such splendour, although it is said that the carved figure of a seated man with crutches in the central arch of the central doorway represents the unnamed architect.

One fact is certain: the history of the basilica dates back to 828 when two merchants returned to Venice from Alexandria in Egypt, carrying with them the relics of **St Mark**. It is thought that the ruling doge at the time, **Giustiniano Parteciaco**, had commissioned the theft to enhance his prestige and that of Venice. He built a church and shrine in honour of the Evangelist, basing it on the **Church of the Apostles in Constantinople**, then the richest city in Christendom, and St Mark became the patron of the city.

Throughout the Golden Age of Venice, St Mark's was the **Doge's Chapel**, subject to the authority of the Republic, continually embellished over the centuries by various doges eager to demonstrate their power and wealth. When, in the twelfth century, Venice was divided into six administrative districts (*sestieri*), it was only appropriate to name this central part of the city where the power was concentrated San Marco.

> *The church in Venice is something more than all things bright and beautiful. It is descended from Byzantium, by faith out of nationalism: and sometimes to its high ritual in the Basilica of St Mark there is a tremendous sense of an eastern past, marbled, hazed and silken.*

Jan Morris, *Venice*, 1960

The Maestro di Cappella di San Marco was the most prestigious musical appointment in all of Italy, and was variously held by such great composers as Gabrieli, Cavalli and Monteverdi. St Mark's eventually became the city cathedral in 1807.

The striking cross-shaped basilica is the third church to stand on this site, and its original structure is largely eleventh century. Initially, the building was plain brick. The process of adorning the church in gold, mosaics and marble took a further two centuries of painstaking work. Now, with its quincunx of domes, its acres of mosaics and the conglomeration of architectural styles, it is considered the most glorious Byzantine building in the Western world.

However, over the centuries, reactions to St Mark's have been mixed. In 1645, John Evelyn wrote in his *Diary*: 'This church is in my opinion much too dark and dismal'; Charles de Brosses, in 1739, thought it 'low in structure, very sombre, in miserable taste, both within and without'; Jan Morris (*Venice*) called it 'a barbaric building, like a great Mongolian pleasure pavilion, or a fortress in Turkestan'; while Mark Twain likened it to 'a warty bug out for a stroll'.

Getting there: Piazza San Marco. Tel: 041 5225697. Main part of church open: daily 0945–1730; Museo Marciano (Loggia dei Cavalli) open: daily 0945–1600. Admission: free. Treasury open: daily 0945–1600. £. Golden Altar Screen open: daily 0945–1600. £. Services are held eight or nine times a day so avoid these times. Guided tours in English twice a week in summer months. Vaporetto: San Marco or San Zaccaria.

Basilica San Marco II

The façade

The main façade is one of the most striking features of the basilica, with its masterful balance of columns, arches, marble slabs and mosaics depicting scenes from the lives of **Jesus** and **St Mark**. One mosaic (on the left-hand side) recreating *The Bringing of St Mark's Body to the Basilica*, reputedly smuggled out of Alexandria under slices of pork in a barrel, represents the earliest known depiction of St Mark, and it shows the first basilica. Note also the exquisite carvings on the triumphal arches of the central doorway. These provide a valuable insight into thirteenth-century city life, especially the **central arch**, which portrays such seasonal Venetian labours as fishing (lower right) and shipbuilding (lower left).

Spanning the façade, the **loggia** is surmounted by replicas of the four famous St Mark's horses. The gilded bronze originals are now protected inside the basilica (*see below*). Of the six cupolas in the **atrium** illustrating scenes from the Old Testament, the **Genesis cupola** (far right) is particularly striking, portraying *The Creation* in concentric circles.

❝ ... little cubes of crystal gleam here and there like the sunlit sea: the outlines of the figures tremble in their golden field ... the angels unfold the long wings of azure and purple which an implacable mosaic holds to the wall ... ❞

Théophile Gautier,
***Voyage en Italie*, 1852**

The interior

The glittering interior – dark and exotic, smothered in gold, marble and mosaics – will take your breath away. Many of the original mosaics have been replaced in the last two centuries, but the church remains as magnificent as ever. When illuminated, the entire church is radiantly bathed in golden light, described by W B Yeats as 'God's holy fire'. The most lavish mosaics grace the three main domes: the **Pentecost Dome** (nearest the door) portrays the *Descent of the Holy Spirit* in the form of a dove; the Ascension Dome in the centre shows *Christ in Majesty*; and the Dome of Emmanuel (in the sanctuary) shows *Christ with Prophets*. Other dazzling mosaics depict scenes from the lives of Christ, St Mark and various other saints.

As you gaze in awe at the bejewelled ceiling, don't overlook the swirling, multicoloured patterns of glass, marble and porphyry that make up the magnificent, undulating pavement. In the nineteenth century, the authorities began a massive replacement project to level the floor, until a British architect managed to block it by persuading them that the wave-like surface of the floor was a deliberate attempt to imitate the sea.

Treasures

The basilica has been called 'the world's greatest stolen property office' as, over the centuries, it has been filled with booty from every corner of the city's once far-flung empire – capitals from Sicily, porphyry from Syria, columns from Alexandria and sculpture from Constantinople. Its most precious treasures include the Byzantine-style Pala d'Or, a jewel-spangled golden altarpiece, adorned with enamels and over 3 000 precious stones. St Mark's remains are said to lie beneath the high altar, although they were probably destroyed during a fire in 976.

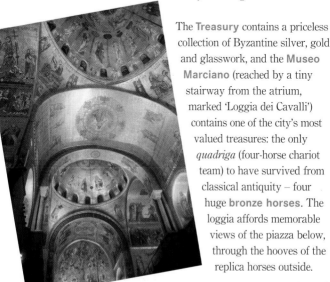

The Treasury contains a priceless collection of Byzantine silver, gold and glasswork, and the Museo Marciano (reached by a tiny stairway from the atrium, marked 'Loggia dei Cavalli') contains one of the city's most valued treasures: the only *quadriga* (four-horse chariot team) to have survived from classical antiquity – four huge bronze horses. The loggia affords memorable views of the piazza below, through the hooves of the replica horses outside.

Campanile di San Marco

Piazza San Marco. Tel: 041 5224064. Open: daily 0900–1900 (0930–1545 in winter months). ££. Vaporetto: San Marco or San Zaccaria.

" *On Monday early, the Campanile was resplendent in the sunshine … Suddenly I saw it slowly sink directly downward behind a line of roofs, and a dense grey dust rose in clouds … I ordered my gondolier to the Piazzetta. On arrival the sight was pitiful. Of that splendid shaft all that remained was a mound of white dust …* "

– report in *The Times* by an American architect, July 1902

St Mark's Bell Tower, fondly nicknamed the *paròn di casa* ('man of the house'), offers visitors the best panoramas of Venice. It was from here that **Galileo** first demonstrated his telescope in 1609, and it is easy to see why. From the top, almost 100m (325ft) above the piazza, you can see for miles – over the city, the lagoon and, on a clear day, the Alps.

The Campanile has always been a reference point for sailors. The roof of the first tower, built in 888, was covered with mirrored slabs so they would gleam in the sun and be visible from afar. At night, wood was burned in the belfry for the same reason. The existing tower was constructed in 1511. However, suddenly, on 14 July 1902, it fell down. Remarkably, the only casualty was the custodian's cat. The tower was immediately rebuilt according to the original design. Even **Sansovino**'s beautiful loggia at the base of the tower, decorated with his finest statues, was painstakingly reconstructed by piecing together the fragments. It now forms the entrance to the tower.

Today, a lift takes visitors to the top. But try to avoid being up there when the five bells chime the hour!

Canal Grande

From vaporetto stop Rialto to San Marco.

The view along the final stretch of the canal – from the Rialto round La Volta ('the curve') and along to St Mark's Square – is one of the grandest. Here, you can see some of the finest palaces of Venice. Several contain some of the city's most celebrated hotels, some are now museums and galleries, others are luxury apartments, many are famed for their celebrity links. **Palazzo Mocenigo**, for instance (formed by four palaces linked together just before La Volta, opposite San Tomà *vaporetto* pier), served as lodgings to **Lord Byron** who, at times, would swim from the Lido up the Grand Canal to his house. The elegant, cream-coloured **Palazzo Grassi**, the last great palace to be constructed on the canal (just before San Samuele landing-stage, with its own pier), is one of the most imposing *palazzi* on this stretch of water. It was bought by Fiat in 1984 and converted into a centre for art exhibitions *par excellence*.

The Grand Canal has always been an endless source of inspiration to artists and writers. Two palaces beyond Accademia Bridge, **Monet**, **Whistler** and **John Singer Sargent** all had studios in **Palazzo Barbaro**, **Robert Browning** gave recitations in the library and **Henry James** wrote *The Aspern Papers* here. Sculptor **Canova** had a studio in pretty **Casetta delle Rose**, one of the smallest houses on the canal (seven mansions on from Palazzo Barbaro, set back in tiny gardens), while his jealous mistress purchased the house opposite to keep an eye on him.

93

Over-zealous tour guides describe the tiny, fairy-tale, pink-fronted **Palazzo Fasan** (three buildings after the Hotel Gritti Palace, with lacy, circular-patterned balconies) as the fictional 'House of Desdemona' from Shakespeare's *Othello*. Just prior to the San Marco landing-stage, guests at the Gothic **Palazzo Giustinian** (between Hotels Bauer Grünwald and Monaco e Grand Canal), once a hotel, included **Verdi**, **Turner**, **Proust** and **George Eliot**. The celebrated **Harry's Bar** (at the landing-stage; *see page 106*) makes a fitting end to your voyage.

Museo Civico Correr

Piazza San Marco (entrance in Ala Napoleonica). Tel: 041 5225625.
Open: Nov–Mar, daily 0900–1700; Apr–Oct, daily 0900–1900. ££. Café
and bookshop. Vaporetto: *San Marco.*

Make this, Venice's principal historical museum, your first
port of call. Once you have a grasp of Venice's colourful
history you will find subsequent walks around town all the
more rewarding.

> ❝ *'Tis ridiculous to see how*
> *these ladys crawle in and*
> *out of their gondolas by*
> *reason of their* zoccoli, *and*
> *what dwarfs they appeare*
> *when taken down from their*
> *wooden scaffold.* ❞
>
> **John Evelyn on ladies'**
> **footwear,** *Diary*, **1640**

The museum runs above the arcades on
the west and south sides of **Piazza San
Marco**. It is named after the wealthy
abbot **Teodoro Correr**, whose countless
paintings and documents, bequeathed to
the city in 1830, form the core of the
collection. The wide marble staircase was
once the grand entrance to **Napoleon**'s
prestigious palace, and the first rooms of
the museum display the glorious neo-
classical décor of the Ala Napoleonica,
fittingly enhanced by works of the great neo-classical
sculptor **Antonio Canova**.

The museum continues on two floors of the **Procuratie
Nuove**, where the entire *piano nobile* (first floor) is
devoted to the history of the **Venetian Republic** and the
Risorgimento. Several rooms are dedicated to the figure of
the doge, including a rare fifteenth-century *zoia* (doge's cap)
and its white silk *rensa* (under-bonnet), and a fragment
of tapestry with a doge's portrait – once part of the altar
frontal donated by each doge, after his election, to the
Basilica of St Mark. The remaining rooms contain a variety
of naval exhibits, maps and globes, arms, furnishings,
musical instruments, assorted versions of the Lion of St
Mark, and coins produced in the neighbouring mint.

Upstairs, a further 20 rooms of art and sculpture provide
vivid insights into Venetian life and art from the fourteenth
to sixteenth centuries through such artists as **Veneziano**,
Vivarini, **Montagna** and **Lotto**. Look out for the **Bellini
salon** with works by three members of this great Venetian
family, and the infamous *Two Venetian Ladies* by **Carpaccio**,
popularly known as *The Courtesans* because of their
saucy low-cut dresses. The most eccentric fashion displayed

in the museum, however, is the extraordinary *zoccoli*: foot-high platform shoes once worn by upper-class women and prostitutes.

Finally, be sure to see the **social games section**, with its paintings of boat parades and carnival scenes, its models of human pyramids (tests of balance and agility which sometimes took place on boats), and noblemen's games practised inside the *ridotti* (aristocratic gaming houses), such as *sbaraglino* (today known as backgammon) and *biribissi* (the precursor of roulette).

Palazzo Contarini del Bovolo

Corte Contarini del Bovolo. Tel: 041 2702464. Open: Apr–Oct, daily 1000–1800; closed during winter months. £. Vaporetto: *Sant'Angelo.*

Palazzo Contarini boasts a unique example of Venetian architecture: an **external spiral staircase**. In the late fifteenth century, Pietro Contarini decided to enlarge his home and added a series of loggias to each floor, linked together by an elegant round tower, which contains the staircase. This graceful swirl of white stone and brick, with its delicate lace-like arches, so caught the imagination of city-dwellers that they nicknamed the palace 'Contarini del Bovolo' ('snail shell' in Venetian dialect).

95

You will find the palace hidden in a maze of alleyways off **Campo Manin**. Visit during the day to enjoy the view from the top of the tower, or see it at its best – by moonlight.

Palazzo Ducale I

*The Doge's Palace is without doubt the grandest of all
Venetian palaces, and for centuries the only building
entitled to the name* palazzo. *The others were simply
called Ca', short for 'Casa'. For nearly a millennium, until
the fall of the Republic in 1797, this was the very nerve
centre of La Serenissima, the seat of its government
and home to its rulers, strategically situated on the
lagoon at the point where Venice surveys the Adriatic.*

The role of the doge

The doge was the supreme magistrate of La Serenissima,
the glorious Venice of the Republic. He was elected by an
assembly of citizens, and remained in office for life. The
first doge, **Paulo Anafesto**, was appointed in 697.

" *'Finally the old Doge
arrives, wearing his
golden Phrygian cap,
in a long cassock all
of gold and an ermine
cape, between three
servants who look
after his train…
he is a handsome,
well-built man …
You might think him
the grandfather of
this whole generation,
he is so affable
and kindly.* "
**Johann Wolfgang von
Goethe**, *Italian Journey*,
1816–29

As Venice gradually achieved independence
from **Byzantium**, the figure of the doge became
increasingly important. He always came from an
influential family and would invariably try to hand
the position, with all its power and glory, on to
his descendants. As a result, various bodies were
formed to limit the doge's control: the **Quarantia**
dealt with legal issues, the **Senate** focused on
political matters and, in 1310, the **Council of
Ten** (nicknamed the 'Terrible Ten') was founded
to investigate conspiracies against the Republic.

Despite this reduction in the doge's power, there
was a gradual increase in the magnificence of his
appearance. For state events he would wear fine
scarlet robes adorned with jewelled clasps and
ermine. The distinctive head-dress (*zoia*) also
became more elaborate, made with gold-trimmed
velvet and studded with precious stones. From
the twelfth century on, he also used the title
'Serenissimo'.

The palace

The first doge's 'palace' here, built in 814, was little more than a fortified castle, but over the centuries the palace was continually rebuilt, enlarged and embellished by all the leading architects of the day. The end result, as seen today – a gracious Gothic structure of gleaming pink marble – dates mainly from the fourteenth and fifteenth centuries, and is particularly striking for its **symmetrical portico** and **lace-like white stone arcades**.

Intricate sculptures grace each corner of the palace, including *The Judgement of Solomon* (near the basilica) and *Adam and Eve* (at the opposite corner). Above one entrance to the palace is a statue of **Doge Francesco Foscari** kneeling before a winged lion, the symbol of St Mark, and of Venice itself.

97

The grand Renaissance courtyard within was a late addition – a grand stage for coronation ceremonies. The **Scala dei Giganti** (Giants' Stairway) is named after the two colossal statues of Mars and Neptune at the top, symbolising the city's domination of land and sea. The **Scala d'Oro** (Golden Stairs) nearby – a magnificent white-and-gold stairway – was designed by **Sansovino** to provide a fittingly splendid entrance to the palace's rooms.

Getting there: Piazzetta San Marco. Tel: 041 5204287. Open: Nov–Mar, 0900–1700; Apr–Oct, 0900–1900 (last admission 90 minutes before closing). £££ (the accompanying audio-guide is thoroughly recommended). Vaporetto: San Zaccaria.

Palazzo Ducale II

The interior

Once inside the labyrinthine palace, you will be dazzled by its grandeur. Some of its finest paintings are in the **Sala di Antecollegio**, including Veronese's *Rape of Europa*, and Tintoretto's *Bacchus and Ariadne* – considered by many his supreme achievement. Together, Veronese and Tintoretto produced the remarkable frescoed ceilings in the **Sala del Collegio** and the **Sala del Senato o Pregadi**. In the **Sala del Consiglio dei Dieci** which follows, the Council of Ten would assemble to judge enemies of the Republic, based on the letters of accusation dropped into the sinister **Bocca di Leone** ('Lion's Mouth') letterbox in the antechamber.

Following the doge's private apartments, the grandiose **Sala del Maggio Consiglio** contains Tintoretto's *Paradise*, reputedly the largest oil painting in the world. Around the walls are portraits of the first 76 doges, with the exception of **Marin Falier**, the only doge to be executed, for treason, in 1355. His portrait is concealed by a black curtain.

The prisons

A series of bare corridors and stairways leads across the **Ponte dei Sospiri** (Bridge of Sighs, *see pages 116–17*) to the prison cells of the adjoining **Palazzo delle Prigioni**. Petty offenders were put in the stifling *piombi* or 'lead' cells under the eaves of the palace. It was from here that **Casanova** made his daring escape through a hole in the roof in 1755. Hardened criminals were placed in the windowless *pozzi* ('wells'), the waterlogged dungeons at ground level, where some of their graffiti can still be seen.

To find out more about the prisons, the torture chamber and state inquisitors' rooms, join the **Itinerari Segreti** ('Secret Itinerary': *1030 and 1200, except Wed, in Italian, English or French; tickets must be reserved in advance on 041 5224951; £££*) which explores the maze of hidden alleys and secret passageways of the palace not covered by the main palace tour. These 'itineraries' last one and a quarter hours.

Piazzetta San Marco

If St Mark's Square is Venice's living room, this adjoining small square, outside the palace and overlooking the lagoon, is the front door and the sea entrance to San Marco and the palace. Two granite columns, one surmounted by a stone **Lion of St Mark**, the other by **St Theodore** (the first patron saint of the city), once marked the ceremonial entrance to the city. Locals consider it unlucky to walk between them as, during the days of the Republic, this was the location of public executions.

> *This deeply original building is of course the loveliest thing in Venice ... Enter at about one o'clock, when the tourists have flocked off to lunch ... All the history of Venice, all its splendid stately past, glows around you in a strong sea-light.* **"**
>
> **Henry James**

The architectural masterpiece overlooking the piazzetta is the **Libreria Sansoviniana**, described by **Palladio** as the finest building since antiquity. It now houses the prestigious library of St Mark. In the neighbouring **Zecca** (Mint), also designed by Sansovino, all the gold and silver of the Republic were produced – shiny coins called *zecchini* (the origin of our word 'sequin'). The **Giardinetti Reali** ('Royal Gardens') here, created by **Napoleon** to improve his view from the Procuratie Nuove (*see page 100*), provide welcome greenery along the waterfront.

Piazza San Marco

Vaporetto: *San Marco or San Zaccaria.*

There is nowhere in the world quite like St Mark's Square. Here, at the very heart of Venice, you will find the renowned basilica and bell-tower, the Corror museum, the magnificent Doge's Palace and some of the city's most famous cafés. From sunrise to nightfall, it is *the* place to people-watch as children feed the pigeons, orchestras serenade the shoppers, and flag-waving tour guides sweep groups of camera-clicking tourists from one sight to the next. Just about anything goes here – except rock concerts, following the debris left after Pink Floyd's performance here in 1989.

Throughout its long history, the piazza has always been Venice's ceremonial gathering place, the main venue for pageants and processions. It was originally conceived as a vista for the **Doge's Palace**, and later became the great showpiece of the Serenissima, the heartbeat of the city and the embodiment of its dreams and aspirations. When **Doge Agnello Parteciaco** built the first palace here in 814, the square was tiny with orchards and vines and a canal running through the middle. Over the centuries, the square developed, and now it boasts some of the city's finest buildings, all of which were once connected to the government of the Republic.

The Procuratie

The square is bounded by the Procuratie, former offices of the Republic's administration. The **Procuratie Vecchie** (along the north side of the square), originally dating from 1100 but rebuilt following a fire in the sixteenth century, housed the Procuratori di San Marco (Procurators of St Mark's) – the nine magistrates who, after the doge, were the most important people in the city. After their investiture ceremony in the basilica, each procurator would distribute bread to the poor and wine to the gondoliers, and then be allotted an apartment here. On the southern side of the square, the **Procuratie Nuove** were completed in the seventeenth century. They became the **Royal Palace** under the rule of **Napoleon** and now contain various cultural institutes and the Museo Corror (*see pages 94–5*).

Napoleon also added the **Ala Napoleonica**, or Procuratie Nuovissime ('even newer'), facing the basilica. This unified the square architecturally and prompted his famous description of the square as 'the most elegant drawing room in Europe'. It is the only square in Venice called a 'piazza' (the others are merely *campi*, or 'fields'). Unfortunately, it is one of the first places in the city to suffer at *acqua alta* (high tide), but even then, daily life goes on as normal, with everyone picking their way across the duck-boards set up across the flooded square.

> " At night ... it seemed to me that the vast square of the winged lion was a single blaze of merry light and that the whole arcade was bustling with people, while other crowds enjoyed themselves in the splendid coffee houses looking on to the square ... When the bronze giants struck midnight, it seemed that all the life and animation of the city was gathered here ... "

Charles Dickens (1812–70)

Historic cafés

Under the arches of the Procuratie are some of the city's most elegant shops and cafés. The first coffee shops opened here in the seventeenth century. Considered highly fashionable places to meet business contacts, gamble, discuss art and literature or simply to chat, there were 27 in the square alone, all with such patriotic names as 'Queen of the Sea', 'Coach of Fortune' and, most famously, 'Venice Triumphant' – now named **Café Florian** (after its founder). It is said that Italy's greatest lover, **Casanova**, after escaping from his prison cell in the Doge's Palace, stopped here for a coffee before fleeing the city. Café Florian was also the favourite haunt of Venetian patriots during the Austrian occupation, while the occupiers patronised **Café Quadri** opposite.

With their expansive terraces, private orchestras and white-frocked waiter service, these two coffee houses still have undeniable charm today as the site of many a historic meeting. Sadly, though, their exorbitant prices limit most people to just one *espresso*.

> " *I can still see the pigeons at Saint Mark's.*
> *The square is silent, the morning is resting.*
> *Lazily, into the sweet fresh air I throw*
> *My songs like so many pigeons into the blue,*
> *Then I call them back*
> *And add a new rhythm to their plumage.* "

– from *Venedig* in *Nietzsches Werke*
by Friedrich Nietzsche (1844–1900)

The Torre dell'Orologio

The tower is currently being restored by Geneva-based watchmaker, Piaget.

On the north side of the piazza, the Torre dell'Orologio (Clock Tower) is a marvel of Renaissance chronometry. Not only does this beautiful gold and blue enamel clock tell the time, it also matches the signs of the zodiac with the phases of the moon and the sun. It was designed to inform sailors of the tides and the best months for sailing. Legend has it that the Venetians were so proud of their unique clock that they gouged out the eyes of the clockmakers who made it, to prevent them from constructing a replica elsewhere.

At the top of the tower, two large bronze Moors strike the hour on a massive bell, and a Madonna and Child sit in a niche above the clock face. During **Ascension Week**, crowds gather on the hour to watch one of the small side doors open and the figures of the Magi walk in procession past the statue, bow and disappear through the other small door. Just above them stands the winged **Lion of St Mark**, the grand symbol of the Serenissima. Two further lions, made of red marble, can be seen guarding the well in the tiny square beside the Clock Tower (adjoining Piazza San Marco), aptly named the **Piazza dei Leoncini**.

The archway here (beneath the Clock Tower) marks the start of the **Mercerie**, a series of streets which once connected St Mark's, the centre of religious and political power, with Rialto, the centre of trade. Today it forms the city's main shopping drag.

Pigeons

The presence of countless pigeons in the square dates back to the time when some were given to the doge as a gift. They escaped, and sought refuge among the vaults of the basilica. The doge decreed that, as they had sought the protection of St Mark, they should be cared for and not recaptured. To this day the portly pigeons are fed around 0900 daily at the city's expense.

San Salvatore

Campo San Salvatore. Open: daily 0900–1200, 1600–1900. Vaporetto: *Rialto*.

Even though San Salvatore is one of the finest Renaissance churches in Italy, it attracts only a modest flow of visitors. It once had a rather different reputation, however. According to a report dated June 1771, 'the Church of San Salvatore is being defiled by the mixed crowds of women who go there, not to hear mass, but to be seen and accosted. God-fearing persons frequently remark that this church has turned into a brothel.'

> " *The Venetians are not quite so religious as you might suppose from their multitude of churches and their mystical origins.* "
>
> **Jan Morris, *Venice*, 1960**

Today, hidden behind a florid baroque façade, the lofty interior is principally admired for its architecture (in particular its unique geometrical design which combines **three domed Greek crosses**), its clean, simple lines and the elegant decorative effect of the soft-toned greys and white. Two important Titians – *The Transfiguration* on the high altar, beautifully illuminated as the focal point of the church, and *The Annunciation* (third altar on the right) – are further good reasons to leave the busy Mercerie and step into the calm of San Salvatore.

Santo Stefano

Campo Santo Stefano. Open: Mon–Sat 1000–1700; Sun 1300–1700. Admission: free; sacristy: £. Vaporetto: *Sant' Angelo or San Samuele*.

Few churches have such a bloody history as Santo Stefano. Deconsecrated six times because of the murder and violence that took place here, its gloomy interior befits its past. But look closer and beneath the **glorious ship's-keel roof**, and you will find the inside is richly painted and colourfully decorated with red and white marble columns, floral frescos and intricate patterns of inlaid marble. Here also lie the tombs of composer **Gabrieli** and **Doge Morosini** (the last great Venetian military commander, best known for blowing up the Parthenon), and, in the sacristy, a collection of treasured paintings, including three late works by **Tintoretto**. The campanile has a characteristic Venetian tilt.

Campo Santo Stefano, second only to St Mark's Square in size and importance, is flanked by striking *palazzi* built by some of the Republic's most noble families. It was also the address of some notable courtesans and, until the nineteenth century, the scene of bull-baiting spectacles.

Teatro La Fenice

Campo San Fantin. Tel: 041 5210161 (Palafenice booking office). Closed indefinitely. Vaporetto: *Santa Maria del Giglio.*

As you pass by what is at present a massive building site, spare a thought for the famous early nineteenth-century opera house of Venice, one of the oldest and most beautiful theatres in Europe, which once stood here. Venice was the first city to have public opera performances, and the world premières of **Verdi's *Rigoletto*** and ***La Traviata***, and, more recently, **Stravinksy's *The Rake's Progress*** and **Britten's *Turn of the Screw***, were staged here.

Unfortunately, the legendary opera house was utterly destroyed by fire on 29 January 1996. More than a year later, two electricians were sentenced for arson. It was by no means the first time Venice's opera house has burnt down though, hence the name Fenice, or 'phoenix'. The original Fenice burnt to the ground in 1836, and it had been built to replace **Teatro San Benedetto**, Venice's first opera house, which also burnt down, in 1774.

The opera house will eventually be reconstructed, but progress is slow owing to controversy over its rebuilding. In the meantime, La Fenice opera company is operating from a marquee, the **Palafenice**, on **Tronchetto**, one of the islands in the lagoon.

Bars, cafés and restaurants

Antico Martini
Campo San Fantin 1983. Tel: 041 5224121. £££. Open: Wed–Mon 1900–2330. The after-theatre stop *par excellence* until neighbouring La Fenice burnt down, but still frequented by celebrities for its refined local cuisine and upstairs piano bar (*open: 2200–0200*).

Ai Do Ladroni
Campo San Bartolomeo 5362. Tel: 041 715736. £. Open: Mon–Sat 0800–2400. A simple, friendly *osteria* right by the Rialto Bridge, with delicious homemade pasta and a fun crowd. Late at night, it takes on a pub feel.

Da Ivo
Ponte dei Fuseri 1808. Tel: 041 5285004. £££. Open: Mon–Sat 1200–1430, 1900–2345. Booking essential. This charming, candlelit restaurant specialises in meat dishes, grilled on olive wood. The Florentine T-bone steak is to die for.

Vino Vino
Ponte della Veste 2007a. Tel: 041 5237027. ££. Open: Wed–Mon 1030–2400. A typical, cosy *osteria* with wooden tables, paper place-mats and wholesome Venetian cooking. The adjoining bar has tasty *cicchetti* (tapas-style snacks) and a large selection of Italian and imported wines.

Alla Botte
Calle San Bartolomeo 5482. Open: Fri–Wed 1000–2000. A real locals' bar – small, dark and crowded, hidden off the tourist track behind the *campo*.

Gelateria Paolin
Campo San Stefano. Open: daily 0800–2200. One of the best ice-cream cafés in town.

Harry's Bar
Calle Vallaresso 1323. Open: daily 1030–2300. The original 'Harry's Bar', the most famous bar in Venice, thanks to Ernest Hemingway, who would stop off here regularly for a 'Bellini' (one-third peach juice, two-thirds *prosecco*). Be warned, however: the prices are a rip-off … but it's a once-in-a-lifetime experience.

Upmarket cafés

Drinking coffee in St Mark's Square is another once-in-a-lifetime experience (*see page 102*). *The* places to go are **Florian** (*closed: Thur*) and **Quadri** (*closed: Mon*), legendary cafés with private orchestras and sunny terraces, immortalised by many film directors and frequented in their heyday by the likes of **Byron**, **Dickens**, **Goethe** and **Proust**.

Shopping

The alleyways surrounding St Mark's Square are bursting with shops. In the narrow streets you will find delightful specialist boutiques, while the glittering main thoroughfares (Calle Larga XXII Marzo, Calle dei Fabbri, Salizzada San Moisè) contain Armani, Prada, Versace and all the big names in Italian design (see page 167 *).*

Araba Fenice
Calle dei Barcaroli 1822. Sophisticated ladies' fashions by a local Venetian designer.

Bevilacqua
Fondamenta Canonica 337b. A treasure trove of luxurious fabrics, tapestries, braiding and brocades, antique and modern, by the leading name in Venetian textiles.

Bottega Veneta
Calle Vallaresso 1337c. Chic, trendy shoes, bags and matching accessories, made in Vicenza.

Chicco Guardaroba
Mercerie dell'Orlogio 217. Designer clothing for kids.

Codognato
Calle Seconda de l'Ascensione 1295. Venice's oldest jewellery shop.

Fiorella
Campo Santo Stefano 2806. Go here for the wackiest fashions in town, with clothes modelled by mannequins of former doges dressed in drag, complete with high heels and lipstick.

Pasticceria Marchini
Ponte San Maurizio 2769. Reputedly the best bakery in town, with a stunning choice of pastries, cakes and biscuits – even chocolate gondolas and masks for carnival.

Nightlife

For late-night bars try the **Devil's Forest** (*Calle Stagneri 5185; open Mon–Sat 0815–0100*), a lively Irish pub popular for backgammon and chess with a good selection of draught and bottled beers, or **Haig's Grill** (*Campo Santa Maria del Giglio 5277*), a smart cocktail bar that serves till 0300 during the summer.

La Fenice
Until La Fenice is rebuilt, the opera company is performing its concert and opera series in a marquee, the Palafenice, on Tronchetto, an island beyond Piazzale Roma and the Stazione Marittima. The box office is in Campo San Luca (*tel: 041 5210161*).

Teatro Goldoni
Calle Goldoni 4650b. Tel: 041 5205422. Venice's main theatre (*see page 177*).

Floods

Whatever anyone says, Venice is still sinking. From the outset, having chosen such an unlikely place to build a city, Venetian inhabitants were faced with the problem of how to keep it from sinking – a dilemma which still haunts their descendants today.

> " *Venice, lost and won,*
> *Her thirteen hundred years*
> *of freedom done,*
> *Sinks, like a sea-weed*
> *Into whence she rose!* "
>
> **Lord Byron, *Childe Harold's Pilgrimage*, 1812–18**

Flood reports date back as early as 855, with 'water invading the whole city, penetrating the houses and the churches'. During the Serenissima Republic, a special **Magistrato alle Acque** (Water Magistrate) was appointed (the position still exists), and he blocked off two of the lagoon's original five openings and constructed long sea-walls as protection against the Adriatic tides.

The twentieth century saw the situation deteriorate. In November 1966, Venice's worst-ever flood pushed water levels 2m (6 1/2 ft) above normal, causing inestimable damage to the city. 'On that single night, our city aged 50 years', remarked the mayor. The *acqua alta* (high tide) floods are a regular feature of winter life, but the area of the city affected is three times greater than it was just a century ago.

The cause of the flooding is simple: wind-enhanced high tides, which fill the

lagoon to overflowing. This problem is exacerbated by dredging, shipping lanes and land reclamation (removing the lagoon's marshes – a natural buffer against high tides). The biggest culprit, however, was the extraction of underground water at a rate of 1.6 million litres (350 000 gallons) hourly from the bed of the lagoon to service the mainland factories of **Marghera**, lowering the water table, and with it the city. When extraction was curtailed in 1973, the water table recovered, but Venice did not.

There seems to be no simple solution. In December 1998 the government shelved the costly, controversial MOSE project to lay eighty movable steel dykes at the three entrances to the lagoon. This pleased sceptics and environmentalists, who maintain the answer lies in less dredging and land reclamation. In the meantime,

the flooding of Venice remains a precarious issue. But everyone agrees: the lagoon must be protected in some way if Venice is to be saved from a watery grave.

Castello

Surprisingly few tourists find their way here, to the greenest, most varied and most truly 'Venetian' district.

CASTELLO

Getting there: By water-bus: Since Castello is sandwiched between the Laguna Nord and the Riva degli Schiavoni, there is a wide choice of vaporetti to choose from. Most routes stop at San Zaccaria, the main landing-stage on the Riva degli Schiavoni, including No 82 from the Zattere and Giudecca and No 1, which also stops at Arsenale, Giardini and Sant' Elena. Circular route 41/42 (in an anti-clockwise direction) provides a useful means of circumnavigating the district.

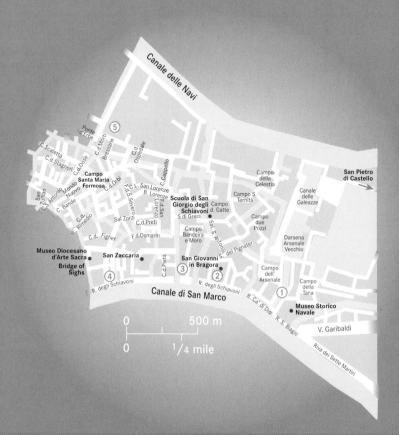

① The Arsenale

Visit Venice's docklands, where no new ships have been launched for generations, but where the crumbling Renaissance warehouses and empty shipyards of La Serenissima's once magnificent maritime hub still stand in ruinous dignity. The fascinating **Museo Storico Navale** nearby will fill you in on its extraordinary naval history. Page 114

② Riva degli Schiavoni

A stroll along the most popular promenade, the Riva degli Schiavoni, is an integral part of any visit to Venice. On sunny days, it is a delight to sit at a waterside café, looking across to the islands of **San Giorgio Maggiore** and **Giudecca**. The glorious views almost compensate for the more commercialised aspect of the quayside, with its souvenir stalls and excursion boats. Page 118

③ Vivaldi at La Pietà

Surely there could be no finer place to hear the legendary *Four Seasons*, or another Vivaldi concerto, than here, in the venue for which the music was written? Venice's great maestro, nicknamed 'the red priest', was choirmaster at the church of La Pietà for nearly 40 years, and today, concerts of his music are staged twice weekly. Page 116

④ Hotel Danieli

Push the boat out and enjoy the meal of a lifetime on the rooftop terrace of the Hotel Danieli. The food and service are everything you would expect of the city's most famous hotel, and the views over the starlit lagoon will make it an evening to remember. Page 115

⑤ Santi Giovanni e Paolo

Marvel at the tombs and extravagant marble mausoleums of many of Venice's great doges and dignitaries and pay your respects at Santi Giovanni e Paolo, the largest of the city's 200 churches, and also its unofficial pantheon. Page 122

Tip

Visiting hours of Venice's sights are often subject to change at short notice. To save disappointment, check with the tourist office for the latest opening hours as soon as you arrive, and don't be surprised to find sections of museums and galleries closed, or chapels containing precious artworks scaffolded off, as ongoing restoration is an eternal feature of the city.

113

Tourist information

There is no tourist information office in this district. The closest one is near St Mark's Square at Calle Larga dell'Ascensione (*see page 87*).

The Arsenale

Italian naval property – public access only during exhibitions. Vaporetto: *Arsenale.*

For seven centuries, this massive dockyard was the maritime powerhouse of the Venetian Republic. Officially founded in 1104 as a small shipyard and dock, it reached its maximum expansion in the sixteenth century when, with over 3 000 workmen, it was producing an astounding two complete galleys a day to create the invincible fleet of warships with which Venice ruled its *stato da mar* (sea state).

The mighty castellated walls and imposing defensive towers of the Arsenale are visible from afar, and its fine entrance is guarded by **four monumental marble lions** – all spoils of war. Peer through the Renaissance gateway to see the massive workshops, foundries and warehouses where up to 150 galleys could be built simultaneously. Though now largely derelict, it is still easy to imagine the Arsenale in its heyday, when the likes of Pero Tafur came this way: 'As one enters the gate there is a great street on either hand with the sea in the middle, and on one side are windows opening out of the houses of the arsenal, and the same on the other side, and out came a galley towed by a boat, and from the windows they handed out to them, from one the cordage, from another the bread, from another the arms, and from another the *balistas* (canons) and mortars … and when the galley had reached the end of the street all the men required were on board, together with the complement of oars, and she was equipped from end to end' (*Travels and Adventures, 1435–1439*).

Hotel Danieli

Riva degli Schiavoni. Tel: 041 5226480. Vaporetto: *San Zaccaria.*

Style and elegance are the hallmarks of the luxurious Danieli, Venice's most famous hotel. This former doge's residence, with its distinctive terracotta Venetian Gothic façade overlooking St Mark's Basin, was constructed in the fifteenth century to demonstrate the wealth and power of the Republic. From the opulent marble lobby, with its golden staircase and Murano chandeliers, to the dreamy bedrooms, with frescoed ceilings and plush antique furnishings, Hotel Danieli has maintained the atmosphere and timelessness of bygone days.

The hotel's modern wing (the Danielino) was added in 1948 on a site where building was prohibited for 800 years, as it marked the spot where **Doge Vitale Michiel II**

> **"** *The beginning of everything was in seeing the gondola-beak come actually inside the door at Danieli's, when the tide was up, and the water two feet deep at the foot of the stairs.* **"**
>
> **John Ruskin, *Works***

was murdered in 1172. The assassin had sheltered in a house in Calle delle Rasse, so accordingly all the houses here were razed to the ground. Unfortunately, the Danielino does little credit to this distinguished hotel.

If you are lucky enough to stay at the Danieli, request a room in the ancient *palazzo* and follow in the footsteps of such notables as **Dickens**, **Wagner**, **Debussy**, **Cocteau** and **Balzac**, all of whom have graced the hotel's prestigious guest list. The Danieli also witnessed the end of the tempestuous affair between **Alfred de Musset** and **George Sand**, who ran off with de Musset's doctor while he lay on his sick bed. In 1959, **Marcel Proust** was so enchanted by the Danieli that he stayed awhile: 'When I went to Venice I found that my dream had become – incredibly, but quite simply – my address.'

La Pietà

*Riva degli Schiavoni. Tel: 041 5222171. Open for concerts only (*see page 177*).*
Vaporetto: *San Zaccaria.*

If hearing music in the place for which it was written is a special joy, then visit La Pietà, the church where from 1703 to 1740 **Antonio Vivaldi** was concert-master. Although ordained a priest, and nicknamed *il prete rosso* because of his red hair, he devoted his life to music, working as a violin teacher and choirmaster at the **Ospedale della Pietà**, the orphanage attached to the church.

The orphanage corresponded to today's music conservatories. All the girls were educated and taught to play a musical instrument. Vivaldi wrote many of his finest pieces for the church, including 454 concertos and the well-known *Four Seasons*. Whenever dignitaries visited, a concert would be staged at La Pietà in their honour, and the choir and orchestra soon became known throughout Europe. However, tastes changed, and by 1740 Vivaldi's music was out of fashion in Venetian circles, so he left to seek work in Vienna. He died a year later and was buried in a pauper's grave.

You can still hear Vivaldi's music played here on **Monday and Thursday evenings**. Unfortunately, this is the only chance to admire the interior of the church, with its precious **Tiepolo** paintings. Once inside, note how the ceiling was designed without corners, to provide optimal acoustics for the concerts.

Ponte dei Sospiri

Rio del Palazzo (best viewed from Ponte della Paglia). Vaporetto: *San Zaccaria.*

After the **Rialto**, the elegant, covered Bridge of Sighs, built of white Istrian stone with baroque ornamentation, is the most photographed bridge of Venice. It was constructed in the early seventeenth century to provide a link between the law courts of the **Doge's Palace** and the **prisons** (*see page 98*).

> " *I stood in Venice, on the Bridge of Sighs; a palace and a prison on each hand.* "
>
> **Lord Byron, *Childe Harold's Pilgrimage*, 1812–18**

The bridge received its popular name only in the nineteenth century, when the **Romantics** imagined the 'sigh heaved by a prisoner fresh from the courtroom of the palace who crosses the canal by this bridge on his way to serve a long sentence in a foul, dank dungeon; through the lattice window the wretch catches sight of the Lagoon, of the island of San Giorgio, of the sky and the sunshine outside' (Alberto Sordi, *Venezia, la luna e tu*, 1958).

Museo Diocesano d'Arte Sacra Venezia

Ponte della Canonica 4312. Tel: 041 5229166. Open: daily 1030–1230. Vaporetto: *San Zaccaria.*

Don't be put off by the muddled nature of the Diocesan Museum of Venetian Sacred Art's collection, for it is actually more of a storeroom than a museum, containing treasures from churches now abandoned or destroyed, works that risk deterioration or that need restoring and, perhaps most surprising of all, goods that have been stolen and retrieved by Italy's special 'art police'.

You can never be entirely sure what you will find here. The paintings change quite frequently, but you should certainly see a superb collection of early twelfth-century religious gold and silverware from **Santa Maria Formosa** and some beautiful marble sculptures stolen from the former **convent of San Clemente** on an outlying island in the lagoon. The thieves strapped rubber tyres over the figures and dragged them along the bed of the lagoon by motorboat. Look closely, and in places you can still see the tyre marks.

The entire collection is housed in a former Benedictine monastery with a charming Romanesque cloister.

Museo Storico Navale

Campo San Biagio. Tel: 041 5200276. Open: Mon–Sat 0845–1330. ££.
Vaporetto: *Arsenale.*

The Historic Maritime Museum is a must for all who are interested in the illustrious history of Venice as one of the world's greatest maritime powers. The extensive collection, housed in an old granary, ranges from models of the ships built in the neighbouring **Arsenale**, the ancient naval base of the Republic (*see page 114*), to human torpedoes used in World War Two. Other highlights include the engine room of *Elettra* – the laboratory-yacht used by **Guglielmo Marconi**, the Bolognese inventor of radio – ancient globes and charts, a special section devoted to the history of the gondola – including **Peggy Guggenheim**'s private craft – and the *pièce de résistance*: the doge's gold-painted ship of state, the *Bucintoro*, although sadly not the original vessel as that was burnt by **Napoleon**. It is, nonetheless, a magnificent copy.

Riva degli Schiavoni

Vaporetto: *San Zaccaria or Arsenale.*

> " *I had rooms on Riva Schiavoni … the waterside life, the wondrous lagoon spread before me, and the ceaseless human chatter came in at my windows …* "
>
> **Henry James, preface to**
> ***The Portrait of a Lady*, 1881**

There is nothing more pleasurable than strolling along the grand Riva degli Schiavoni, the city's principal waterside promenade. It stretches eastwards from the **Doge's Palace** over several bridges (and with frequent name changes en route), past countless souvenir stalls, restaurants and sunny café terraces to the **Giardini Pubblici**, Venice's dusty, unkempt main park and the venue for the world's biggest open-air contemporary art exhibition, held during summer months in odd-numbered years.

The promenade is named after the traders of **Schivonia (Dalmatia)**, one of the first lands to be conquered by the Republic in the early fifteenth century, who used to moor their boats along the quayside here. Thanks to the exceptional views across St Mark's Basin, the Riva has long attracted celebrities: **Petrarch** lived at No 4145, **Henry James** wrote *The Portrait of a Lady* at No 4161 (now **Pensione Wildner**), **Tchaikovsky** composed his Fourth Symphony at No 4171 (now the **Londra Palace**), **Vivaldi** was concert-master at the **church of La Pietà** (*see page 116*), and a host of luminaries stayed at the **Hotel Danieli** (*see page 115*), including **John Ruskin**, who was enchanted by the views over 'the sea covered with ships and churches and the Doge's Palace, the finest building in the world'.

It has always been the city's most important stretch of water, the place where visiting dignitaries landed, by the Doge's Palace. Nowadays, it is a bustling intersection for excursion boats, *vaporetti* and, beyond the Arsenale, naval vessels and ocean-going liners.

San Giovanni in Bragora

Campo Bandiera e Moro. Tel: 041 5205906. Open: Mon–Sat 0900–1100; Mon–Fri 1700–1900. Vaporetto: *Arsenale.*

Vivaldi was baptised in this small parish church on 4 March 1678, an event commemorated by a small plaque on the simple, unadorned brick façade. The composer lived for many years in one of the houses on the quiet *campo*, which, although just behind the well-trodden **Riva degli Schiavoni**, maintains the feel of a local village square.

Inside the lovely late-Gothic interior shelter numerous art treasures beneath an original ship's-keel roof, including *Christ Resurrected* (left of the doorway into the sacristy) and a tranquil *Madonna and Child with Saints* (left of the high altar), both by **Vivarini**, and, over the high altar, the church's greatest treasure: *The Baptism of Christ* by **Cima da Conegliani**, striking for its brilliant colours.

San Pietro di Castello

Campo San Pietro. Tel: 041 2750462. Open: Mon–Sat 1000–1700; Sun 1300–1700. £. Vaporetto: Giardini.

Far from the classic tourist routes in an intimate, time-locked district of fishing boats and greenery, the imposing church of San Pietro di Castello was Venice's cathedral from 1451, until it was displaced in 1807 by St Mark's Basilica.

> *Venice is like eating an entire box of chocolate liqueurs in one go.*
>
> **Truman Capote (1924–84)**

According to legend, the church was founded by **San Magno** in the eighth century, following a dream in which **St Peter** told him to build a church in the eastern part of the city where he found oxen and sheep grazing. More likely, however, is that the cathedral was intentionally constructed in an isolated location to minimise the influence of the Pope and Rome on the Venetian Republic.

San Pietro was also famous for its annual matrimonial fair, where the youths of the lagoon came to select a wife. The girls would dress in white, with their hair loose and their dowry in a little box slung over their shoulder with a ribbon. Once they had all paired off, the bishop would give them a sermon and his blessing, and then the young men would leave to start married life with their brides and their boxes.

The existing church, built to a **Palladian design** in the mid-sixteenth century, stands forlornly in a small grassy square at the far eastern extremity of the city, together with its precariously tilting white bell-tower. Even its run-down cloisters are strewn with washing, fishing nets and dinghies. However, its grand interior bears testimony to its glorious past, its lofty dome just 4m (13ft) smaller than the dome of St Peter's in the Vatican.

San Zaccaria

Campo San Zaccaria. Tel: 041 5221257. Open: daily 1000–1200, 1600–1800. Admission: free; side chapel: £. Vaporetto: San Zaccaria.

Not only is the **striking façade** of San Zaccaria one of the landmarks of early Renaissance Venetian architecture, but the fresco-smothered interior is more like an art gallery than

a church, boasting fine works by **Tintoretto**, **Titian**, **Bellini** and **Van Dyck**.

To the right of the main building is the first church of San Zaccaria (now the side chapel of the main church) and, further right still, a Benedictine convent. The nuns were all young girls of wealthy noble families, often related to the magistrates of the Republic, or the doge. When the girls joined, they brought with them large dowries, enabling the construction of the large new church in 1461. However, life in the convent was not always austere and dedicated only to prayer: during the eighteenth century, it became known for its masked balls and licentious parties. How fitting that the cells are now occupied by the macho Carabinieri police!

San Zaccaria's greatest treasure is undoubtedly Giovanni Bellini's richly coloured, tranquil *Virgin Enthroned* (second altar on the left), considered by many his finest Madonna. The second altar on the right contains the body of **St Zachary**, father of **St John the Baptist**. The adjoining chapel is decorated with vault frescos by Florentine artist **Castagno**, striking for their realism at a time when local artists were still painting in the Venetian style – with bright colours, static figures and gold backgrounds to create a sense of the divine, as in the chapel's polyptychs. Beneath the chapel, the relics of eight doges lie buried in the often-flooded crypt.

Santi Giovanni e Paolo

Campo Santi Giovanni e Paolo. Tel: 041 5235913. Open: Mon–Sat 1000–1700; Sun 1300–1700. Vaporetto: Fondamente Nuove or Ospedale Civile.

Called **San Zanipolo** by Venetians, this is the largest church in Venice, built by Dominican friars in the thirteenth and fourteenth centuries. Its huge dimensions and important role in public affairs put this basilica on a par with **St Mark's** and the **Frari** as the city's three most important sacred buildings.

Legend has it there was once just a simple chapel here until it appeared in a dream to **Doge Tiepolo** surrounded by flowers, doves and angels. The doge immediately built a church of monumental proportions – an imposing Gothic edifice, striking for its architectural austerity.

The church is also the unofficial pantheon of Venice, as it contains numerous tombs of famous Venetians, including fifteen doges. The most grandiose mausoleums mark the final resting place of Doges **Vendramin**, **Marcello**, **Mocenigo** and **Valier**, all created by illustrious sculptors and adorned with works by the most noted Venetian painters. Especially noteworthy are the bright, luminous retable by **Giovanni Bellini** (in the right aisle) and the ceiling frescos by **Veronese** (in the **Rosary chapel**) depicting scenes from the New Testament. The magnificent **stained-glass window** in the right-hand transept was made by the glassmakers of Murano.

> " *What a funny old city this Queen of the Adriatic is! Narrow streets, vast, gloomy marble palaces, black with the corroding damp of centuries and all partly submerged.* "
>
> **Mark Twain (1835–1910)**

The vast *campo* outside is second only to St Mark's Square in magnificence. The plain, red-brick façade of the church is beautifully offset by the dazzling white marble façade of the **Scuola di San Marco**, now the city hospital, with its remarkable *trompe-l'œil* panels. The square has long been a popular venue for ceremonies and celebrations. Also in the square, the statue of **Bartolomeo Colleoni**, the great Renaissance *condottiere* (military leader), by **Verrochio**, is considered among the world's greatest equestrian monuments. Colleoni left his estate to Venice on condition that a statue in his honour be erected in front of St Mark's Basilica. The Republic agreed, waited for him to die, collected the legacy and then erected his statue in front of the Scuola of St Mark instead.

Scuola di San Giorgio degli Schiavoni

Calle dei Furlani. Tel: 041 5228828. Open: Tue–Sun 1000–1230, 1500–1800. ££. Vaporetto: San Zaccaria or Arsenale.

This simple Scuola contains some of **Vittore Carpaccio**'s finest paintings, commissioned by the Schiavoni (Dalmatian) community at the beginning of the sixteenth century. Having received a precious relic of **St George**, the Schiavoni decided to embellish the Scuola with illustrations of his life and those of their patron saints, **Tryphon** and **Jerome**.

The resulting nine canvases count among the great artistic treasures of Venice. Painted on huge linen canvases because the walls were too damp to paint on to directly, the first three tell the story of St George and the dragon, the next three depict episodes in the life of St Tryphon, and the final three tell the story of St Jerome. With their magical scenes of knights, dragons, princesses and lions, they have an undeniably fairytale-like quality, not to mention their rich colours, their fine attention to detail and, whatever the setting, the frequent references to Venetian architecture. Set inside this tiny chapel and saturated with the odour of incense, these enchanting paintings are more moving here than they could ever be in a museum.

Restaurants

Castello contains some of the city's most prestigious hotels, so there is no shortage of sophisticated dining choices. Two of the finest overlook the lagoon, on the Riva degli Schiavoni: **Do Leoni** *(*Hotel Londra Palace; tel: 041 5200533; £££)*, with its delectable Italian and French cuisine, and the rooftop* **Danieli Terrace** *(*Hotel Danieli; tel: 041 5226480; £££)*, serving an imaginative Mediterranean menu.*

Barbanera

Calle delle Bande 5356. Tel: 041 5210717. £. Open: daily 1030–2300. This simple pizzeria-spaghetteria near St Mark's Square is ideal for lunch, with generous helpings, excellent salads and sandwiches, and a huge selection of bottled beers.

Corte Sconta

Calle del Pestrin 3886. Tel: 041 5227024. ££. Open: Tue–Sat 1100–1600, 1800–2400. Booking advisable. An excellent *osteria* near the Arsenale, with a relaxed atmosphere, a pretty courtyard and the freshest of fish. There's no written menu, just a couple of choices per course, depending on the day's catch.

Al Covo

Campiello della Pescaria 3968. Tel: 041 5223812. £££. Open: Fri–Tue 1245–1530, 1930–2400. Booking essential. Formal yet friendly and intimate, this top-class restaurant in a quiet corner of Castello serves such delights as *ravioli di branzino* (sea bass), roast wild teal, and pear and prune cake with cinnamon and grappa sauce.

Al Mascaron

Calle Longa Santa Maria Formosa 5225. Tel: 041 5225995. ££. Open: Mon–Sat 1130–1600, 1900–2400. Booking essential. Charmingly decorated with copper pots, wooden wine casks and old photos of Venice, this tiny *osteria* is always crammed with locals. The menu is simple, the service a little slow, but the food excellent.

Shopping

Perle Veneziane
Ponte della Canonica 4308. Beautiful, affordable costume jewellery made of Venetian glass.

Studio d'Arte
Campo San Zaccaria 4683b. Artist and architect Missiaja's striking watercolours of Commedia dell'Arte characters make a wonderful souvenir of the Venice Carnival.

Trilly
Fondamenta dell'Osmarin 4974. Handmade porcelain dolls and puppets dressed in traditional Venetian costumes – a collectors' paradise.

Vino e Vini
Fondamenta dei Furlani 3301. Thinking of taking home some local wines? Then this is the shop for you, with a wide choice and helpful staff to advise.

Biscuits

The ancient forni pubblici *(public bakeries) once stood in Castello (at Riva Ca' di Dio 2179–2180). Their main function was to supply the nearby Arsenale, and it is here that the biscuit (from* bis-cotto, *meaning 'twice-cooked') was first conceived as a long-lasting staple for the ancient mariners. Today's Venetian favourites include* busolai *(very sweet, and tasting of aniseed); yellow* zaletti, *made with cornmeal, raisins, lemon and vanilla;* buranelli, *not unlike shortbread;* pignoletti, *made from sugar, almonds and pine nuts; and crisp, dry* baicoli, *named after a lagoon fish whose shape it resembles. At carnival time, you will also see* frittelle *doughnuts filled with raisins, cream or* zabaglione, *and wafer-thin* crostoli, *thin flakes of deep-fried pastry dusted with icing sugar.*

Nightlife

There are some excellent bars in Castello to suit all tastes. **Birreria Forst** (*Calle delle Rasse 4540; open: 1030–2345*) is just off the waterfront and popular for a quiet beer. Irish pub **Inishark** (*Calle Mondo Novo 5787; open: Tue–Sun 1700–0130*) is noisy, with live music on Fridays. **La Mascareta** (*Calle Lunga Santa Maria Formosa 518; open: Mon–Sat 1130–1500, 1900–2330*) is one of the few authentic *enoteche* ('wine bars') in Venice. **L'Olandese Volante** (*Campo San Lio 5658; open: Mon–Sat 1000–2400*) has a lively outdoor terrace and is currently the 'in' pub with the local student population.

Messing about in boats

Stand on a bridge over the Grand Canal and you will be amazed at the huge variety of craft that come by: vaporetti, motoscafi, *water-taxis and a host of service boats – police, fire, ambulance, delivery boats, rubbish collectors, hearses and dredgers. With 180 canals covering over 45km (28 miles), everything in Venice is done by boat.*

Stately gondolas, unique to Venice and first recorded in 1094, once numbered 14,000. Today there are fewer than 400, but for centuries they have been made to the same design. They are 10.87m (35 ^{2}/$_3$ ft) in length, with a maximum width of 1.42m (4 ^{2}/$_3$ ft). The hull is asymmetrical – 24cm (9 ^{1}/$_2$ in) wider on the left than the right to assist with steerage – and the bows end in an iron *ferro*, with six prongs representing Venice's six *sestieri*. Each gondola consists of 280 parts made from fir, cherry, walnut, larch, mahogany, oak, lime and elm. According to a sixteenth-century law, seven layers of black lacquer must be applied.

Voga alla Veneziana (Venetian oarsmanship – or rowing standing up) is very skilful, and you can often see gondoliers practising in quiet backwaters (and beginners falling overboard). The best time to see gondolas in action, however, is during one of the city's annual regattas and water festivals.

" *These black gondolas slipping round the canals look like both coffins and cradles, the last and first resting-places of mankind.* **"**

Madame de Staël,
Corrine ou l'Italie,
1806

La Sensa, on the Sunday after Ascension, celebrates Venice's 'Marriage with the Sea'. Originally, the doge sailed in his ceremonial boat, the *Bucintoro* (*see page 118*); today, the mayor takes to the seas to utter the historic vow: 'We wed thee, O sea, in token of true and lasting dominion.' The following Sunday, **La Vogalonga** ('the long row'), a marathon 32km- (20-mile) row, attracts hundreds of vessels from six-manned racing *caorlini* and two-man *gondolini* to simple, flat-bottomed *sandali* (fishing boats).

The most spectacular festivals include the **Festa del Redentore** ('Feast of the Redeemer'; *see page 134*) on the third Sunday in July; the **Regata Storica** ('Historic Regatta') on the first Sunday in September (traditional craft on a streamer-festooned Grand Canal, in Renaissance costume); and on 21 November, the **Festa della Madonna della Salute** (*see page 78*), with a grand votive procession across the Grand Canal to celebrate the city's deliverance from the plague of 1630.

THE LAGOON

The Lagoon

To visit the islands of the lagoon puts Venice into perspective. La Serenissima is not simply a remarkable city born out of the sea, but part of an archipelago of over 40 islands scattered across a vast lagoon.

BEST OF

The Lagoon

Getting there: *For islands south of Venice, Vaporetto No 82 runs from Ferrovia, Piazzale Roma, Zattere, San Zaccaria and other more minor landing-stages. The quickest and most convenient way to reach islands north of Venice (San Michele, Murano, Burano and Torcello) is on motoscafo No 12. Several lines go to the Venetian Lido: Nos 1 and 82, the night boats (marked 'N'), which also ply the length of the Grand Canal, and Nos 6, 14 and 51/52. In summer months, route 61/62 also operates to the Lido from San Zaccaria, with an extra stop at the casino.*

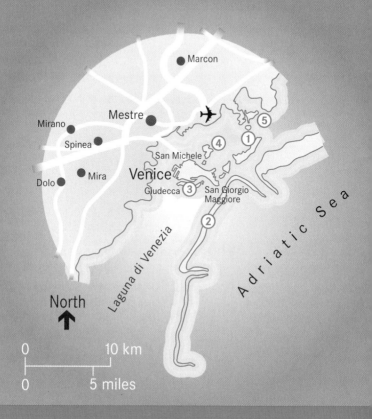

① *Burano*

Burano, the traditional home of fishermen and lace-makers, is without doubt the most vibrant and picturesque of Venetian islands, packed with boats and scores of brightly coloured cottages, and one of the best places to eat freshly caught fish from the lagoon.
Pages 132–3

② *The Lido*

This long, thin, sandy strip of land, belonging neither to Venice nor the mainland, has long been a renowned and elegant sea resort, and is the ideal place to bring children to play on the beach or to escape the mid-summer heat of Venice for a refreshing dip in the cool Adriatic. **Page 135**

③ *Il Redentore and San Giorgio Maggiore*

Be sure to visit these two magnificent churches, which pierce the skyline to the south of Venice – Il Redentore on Giudecca and San Giorgio Maggiore on the island of the same name. Both were designed by the influential neo-classical architect **Andrea Palladio**, and count among the finest churches in the lagoon. **Pages 134 and 138**

④ *Murano*

Ardent shoppers will have a job resisting the sparkling choice of glassware on Murano. Visit the island's **glass museum** first, though, to guide you with your shopping list. **Pages 136–7**

⑤ *Torcello*

The very cradle of Venetian civilisation, this tiny green island with its ancient churches and dazzling mosaics, archaeological museum and fine restaurants, can easily be explored on a gentle half-day trip from Venice, or combined with Burano for a more extended excursion. **Pages 138–9**

Tip

Consider an early-morning boat trip to the islands of Burano and Torcello to experience the scenery of the lagoon at its best – a world of shimmering greens and blues, dotted with islands and semi-submerged sandbanks; a world of profound silence, solitude and sea birds.

131

Tourist information

There is no tourist information office on the islands. The closest one is near St Mark's Square at Calle Larga dell'Ascensione (*see page 87*).

Burano

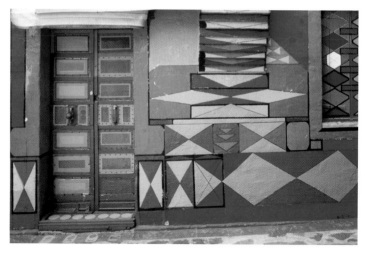

*One of the gems of the lagoon, and certainly the most photogenic island. Thankfully only a manageable number of tourists make it to Burano, less than an hour away from Venice. The main appeal of this pretty little port is undoubtedly its **neat, clean and gaily painted cottages** – brilliant reds, blues, pinks, lilacs, greens and yellows which reflect in the narrow canals. It is so picturesque that on first impression it seems more like a colourful film-set than a real community – an impression heightened by its alarmingly tilted bell-tower.*

The locals – the cheerful Buranelli, who number around 4 000 – are a busy, hard-working folk. There are no buildings of particular architectural value on Burano, although the **church of San Martino** does contain a painting of *The Crucifixion* by **Tiepolo**. Yet by painting the houses in such lively colours, its inhabitants found a way of transforming the entire island into a work of art. Surprisingly, it was the women of the island who did the painting, so that their men-folk could recognise home from afar when they returned from their fishing trips. In the evenings you can still see fishermen awaiting nightfall, preparing their boats and repairing their nets. Today, the islanders live chiefly off fishing, and the fish restaurants here offer some of the finest old-fashioned cooking in the lagoon.

But it is **lace-making** that has made the island of Burano world-famous. The origins of lace-making here are inextricably entwined with a mythical tale of adventure on the high seas. A young sailor, on returning from one of his voyages to distant lands in the fifteenth century, brought his beloved for a bridal veil a piece of beautiful seaweed he had been given by a mermaid. Moved by the beauty of the gift, the girl decided to reproduce it with a needle and thread, and thereby created a fine and fragile material. This beautiful 'lace' rapidly became highly sought after by aristocratic Venetian ladies, and made a considerable contribution to the economy of the Republic.

The initial technique, based on the seaweed design, became known as *punto aria* (the earliest form of needlepoint), and in the sixteenth century various other stitches were devised, including *roselline* (little star-shaped rosettes) and *controtagliato* (with large scrolls). You can learn more of the history and techniques of lace-making on the island in the **Scuola e Museo di Merletto** (School and Museum of Lace-making: *Piazza Galuppi; tel: 041 730034; open: Apr–Sept, Wed–Mon 1000–1700; Oct–Mar, Wed–Mon 1000–1600; ££*), housed in an attractive Gothic *palazzo* in Piazza Galuppi, the island's main square. Sadly, it is rare to see local womenfolk sitting on their doorsteps making lace these days, but you may see a demonstration in the museum.

Shops and stalls in the main street, **Via Baldassarre Galuppi** (named after a local musician), sell all manner of lace products, but beware! If it's cheap, it's probably imported from China.

> *It [the lagoon] is a muted scene, slate-grey, pale blue and muddy green: but in the middle of it there bursts a sudden splurge of rather childish colour, its reflections spilling into the water, and staining these lugubrious channels like an overturned paint-pot. This is the island town of Burano ... a jumble of primary colours shining in the mud.*

Jan Morris, *Venice*, 1960

Giudecca

In the time of the Republic, Giudecca was called the 'Garden Isle', home to a large botanical garden with exotic plants from the Far East and a rose garden with over 180 different species. For a while, before the founding of the ghetto (*see page 28*), it was also a Jewish enclave – hence the name 'Giudecca' (from *giudei*, meaning 'Jews') – and it was also noted for its convents, including one notorious for the amorous exploits of **Casanova**. From the Renaissance onwards, it became a popular place for noble Venetians to build palatial villas in which to spend their summer months.

During the nineteenth century, the island became Venice's industrial inner suburb, with flour mills, factories and breweries. Still today, the island provides a taste of how working Venice really lives, with its children's playgrounds, oar-makers' workshops and boat-builders' yards. Landmarks on this narrow strip of land include the abandoned, fortress-like **Mulino Stuky** (on the western edge of the island), until 1955 Venice's official flour mill but soon to be developed into apartments and a hotel; the **Hotel Cipriani**, certainly one of the world's most exclusive hotels (at the western end of the island); and the **Zitelle church and convent**, designed by **Palladio** in 1570 and today used as a convention centre. Giudecca's *pièce de résistance*, however, is **Il Redentore** – another Palladian construction, built in gratitude at the end of the terrible plague of 1576. Even today a yearly procession on the third Sunday in July marks the **Festa del Redentore** ('Feast of the Redeemer'), with grand parades of boats festooned in bunting, extravagant firework displays, a pontoon bridge connected to the Zattere and a party atmosphere throughout the island.

The Lido

It takes just ten minutes to reach the long, sandy finger of land known as the Lido, one of the largest islands in the lagoon and a thriving seaside resort. The Lido has two shortcomings: cars are allowed, and its atmosphere is far removed from the real Venice. However, it does boast the most glorious sandy beaches complete with old-fashioned wooden bathing huts, fabulous hotels, a swinging nightlife (during the summer season), a casino, and Venice's only golf course.

Tourists first came here for the 'bathing season' as early as 1840, following the advent of sea-bathing, and before long the island became the world's first 'lido', a glitzy seaside resort that was to be imitated across the globe. As a result, smart art nouveau villas and such glorious *fin de siècle* hotels as **Hotel Excelsior** and **Hotel des Bains** sprang up, the latter made famous as the setting for **Thomas Mann**'s *Death in Venice* and the film of the same name (*see page 62*). They remain *the* places to stay on the island.

Today, the Lido remains essentially a seaside holiday resort, sleepy in winter and packed in the summer, when it is also host to the glamorous **International Film Festival** – the oldest film festival in the world, second only to Cannes in prestige, and staged annually in late August/early September since 1932.

" *This [the Lido] was a holiday-place of all holiday places … Too many people in the piazza, too many trunks of humanity on the beach, too many gondolas, too many motor-launches … too many ices, too many cocktails … too much sun … too many cargos of strawberries … too much enjoyment, altogether far too much enjoyment!* "

D H Lawrence,
Lady Chatterley's Lover, **1928**

135

Murano

The famous glass-making centre of Murano resembles a miniature Venice, just a short water-bus ride away, with its handsome houses, canals, bridges and even its own scaled-down Grand Canal.

The island was first settled in the fifth century and was initially economically linked to **Torcello**. Soon it became a lively trading centre and a major port of call for boats in the Adriatic. It was on excellent terms with neighbouring Venice, which allowed it its own administration. It also minted its own coins. The original families of the island enjoyed special privileges, and their names were inscribed in a Golden Book.

Murano first acquired its nickname, '**the glass island**', in 1291 when the glassmakers and their furnaces were moved here from Venice because of the high incidence of fires in a city predominantly built of wood. From then on, the island specialised in glass production, and soon became the most important centre of its kind. Even though many glass factories lie derelict today, Murano maintains the feel of a small working town, and remains *the* place to buy Venetian glass. Many manufacturers offer visitors demonstrations.

> *For you live like sea birds, with your homes dispersed ... across the surface of the waters ... yet you do not hesitate to oppose so frail a bulwark to the wildness of the sea.*
>
> **– letter to Venetian tribunes from Cassiodorus, prefect of King Theodoric, AD 523**

Murano also warrants a visit for its **architectural treasures**. Being so close to Venice, from the fifteenth to the eighteenth centuries Murano was a popular venue for the Venetian upper class to build their holiday homes, with magnificent gardens, orchards and vineyards. Some of these grand mansions remain today. **Palazzo Giustiniani** was once the residence of the Bishop of Torcello. Since 1861 it has housed the **Museo del Vetro** (Museum of Glass: *Fondamenta Giustiniani 8; tel: 041 739586; open: Apr–Oct, Thur–Tue 1000–1700; Nov–Mar, Thur–Tue 1000–1600; ££;* vaporetto: *Museo*), containing over 4 000 pieces of glassware and illustrating the history and development of the Murano glass industry from the fourteenth century to the present day (*see pages 142–3*).

Murano's greatest architectural jewel is the **church of Santi Maria e Donato**, among the oldest in the lagoon. The apse, facing the canal, is especially striking, its brickwork ornately decorated with niches, columns, capitals and parapets of white Istrian stone. Inside is an intricate mosaic pavement depicting birds and animals, and a beautiful apsidal mosaic of a blue-caped Virgin against a golden background.

San Michele

Encased within walls and studded with cypress trees, tiny San Michele is Venice's cemetery – the '**island of the dead**' – centred around the simple fifteenth-century church of San Michele in Isola (*open: daily 0730–1215, 1500–1600*). Until 1807, when **Napoleon** decreed that all burials should be confined here, Venetians were buried in graveyards around the city. Today, its neat rows of graves are a glorious sight – like a giant, colourful yet slightly dishevelled garden, with tombstones smothered in flowers. Famous inmates include poet **Ezra Pound**, composer **Stravinsky** and ballet impresario **Diaghilev** (*graveyard open: Apr–Sept 0730–1800; Oct–Mar 0730–1600; ask for a map at the main entrance*).

San Giorgio Maggiore

The island of San Giorgio Maggiore, directly opposite St Mark's Square, was once known as the **Isle of Cypresses**. Today its predominant feature is a splendid **Benedictine complex**, with its imposing church, the second highest bell-tower in the lagoon, and its monastery – occupied since 1951 by the prestigious **Fondazione Giorgio Cini**, an important cultural centre which regularly stages temporary art exhibitions and international events.

The magnificent neo-classical church (*open: daily 1000–1230, 1430–1630*) is considered one of **Andrea Palladio**'s masterpieces, especially striking for its absence of decoration and for the clean architectural lines of the bright white interior. It is among the most photographed churches in all Venice because its **grandiose white façade** reflects the changing light and mood of the lagoon, and is particularly beautiful at sunset.

The elegant campanile, although not as high as the one in St Mark's Square, affords better views of the lagoon, especially at low tide when you can see the shallowness of the water, and it is easy to pick out the *bricole* – bundles of poles – which mark the shipping channels and narrow inter-island water-bus routes.

Torcello

> *Mother and daughter, you behold them both in their widowhood – Torcello and Venice.*
>
> **John Ruskin, *Works***

The tiny island of Torcello is a 'wild sea moor' (John Ruskin) of salt marshes and sea lavender, with green, sluggish canals and a population of ducks, white egrets and a few dozen inhabitants. There are no *calli*, no *campi*, just a handful of crumbling houses, three restaurants and two bridges. Yet it was on this peaceful, green island that the story of Venice began.

Torcello was the first island in the lagoon to be settled by refugees from the mainland during the barbarian invasions of the fifth century. By the tenth century it had become a thriving political and religious centre with flourishing wool

and salt-mining industries. But, over the centuries, the silting up of its creek and the prevalence of malaria forced many of its inhabitants to flee to nearby Venice, and before long the little island became almost deserted.

All that remains now of its glorious past is a scattering of ancient monuments. The most prestigious is the **Cathedral of Santa Maria Assunta** (*tel: 041 730084; open: Apr–Oct, daily 1030–1730; Nov–Mar, daily 1000–1700; ££*) with its dominant campanile, distinct from afar. Inside, a **stone tablet** dates the original edifice to 639, making it the earliest documented building in the lagoon.

The beautiful twelfth-century mosaics are similar to those in St Mark's Basilica, and were probably created by the same craftsmen. Especially notable are the giant 'comic-strip' mosaic frieze of *The Last Judgement*, staggering in its complexity of detail, and the exquisite *Mater Dolorosa* – a strikingly simple golden depiction of Jesus and Mary holding in her hand a handkerchief to symbolise the tears she will shed for the death of her son.

139

The adjoining **church of Santa Fosca** (*open: daily 1000–1230, 1400–1700*) was first erected in 864 as a martyrium containing the bodies of **St Fosca** and **St Maura**. It was reconstructed in the tenth century on a central Greek cross floor plan with a wooden roof, and surrounded by an **unusual octagonal portico**. The nearby **Estuary Museum** (*open: Apr–Sept, Tue–Sun 1000–1230, 1400–1730; Oct–Mar, Tue–Sun 1030–1230, 1400–1600*) contains valuable archaeological remains of the island and, in the courtyard, the alleged fifth-century throne of **Attila the Hun**.

Cafés and restaurants

Ai Pescatori
*Burano. Via Galuppi 371. Tel: 041
730650. ££. Closed: Wed.* A smart
restaurant with a sunny pavement
terrace, specialising in lagoon fish
dishes, and game in season.

Gatto Nero
*Burano. Fondamenta della Giudecca
88. Tel: 041 730120. ££. Closed: Mon.*
The home cooking of this bright blue
fish restaurant, located on one of
Burano's most picturesque canals, is
popular with locals and visitors alike.

Harry's Dolci
*Giudecca. Fondamenta San Biagio 773.
Tel: 041 5224844. £££. Open: Apr–
Oct; closed: Tue.* At the western end of
Giudecca, with sweeping views across
to the Zattere and refined cuisine. The
prices here are marginally lower than
those of Harry's Bar, the expense-
account flagship near St Mark's
Square, but the Bellinis (*see page 172*)
taste every bit as good.

Ristorante Cipriani
*Giudecca. Giudecca 10. Tel: 041
5207744. £££.* A top-notch restaurant
in a world-famous hotel. The buffet is
immense, and the elegant mirrored
dining room reflects the lagoon.

Bar Gelateria P Garbiso
Lido. Viale Santa Maria Elisabetta 51c.
A popular café, just inland from the
beach, serving coffee, cakes, pastries
and the Lido's best ice-cream.

Da Valentino
*Lido. Corner of Via Sandra Gallo and
Via Fontane. Tel: 041 5260128. ££.
Open: 1230–1430, 1900–2230. Closed:
Mon.* A simple *trattoria* decked out
with gondola *ferri* (*see page 126*)
and oar locks, near the casino.

Busa alla Torre
*Murano. Campo San Stefano 3. Tel:
041 739662. £££.* The reputation of
this tiny fish restaurant in a delightful
tree-shaded square is renowned
well beyond the lagoon. Booking is
recommended, especially in summer.

Valmarena
*Murano. Fondamenta Navagero 31.
Tel: 041 739313. ££.* A sophisticated
restaurant opposite the Museum of
Glass, serving traditional cuisine of the
lagoon (baked scallops, fish *risotto alla
Muranese*) in the beautiful surrounds
of an ancient *palazzo* and gardens.

Locanda Cipriani
*Torcello. Piazza San Fosca 29. Tel:
041 730150. £££. Closed: Tue and
evenings, except Sat.* Yet another chic
Cipriani establishment, in a converted
fisherman's inn at the heart of Torcello.
Arrive in style by private launch from
Piazza San Marco. The set-menu lunch
is particularly good value.

Ponte del Diavolo
*Torcello. Ponte del Diavolo. Tel: 041
730401. £££. Closed: Wed and
evenings, except Sat.* This typically
rustic *osteria* beside an ancient bridge
(said to have been built overnight
by the Devil himself) is primarily a
lunchtime spot, because there is a
problem with mosquitos in the evening
in its charming canalside garden.

Shopping

Domus Vetri d'Arte
Murano. Fondamenta dei Vetrai 82.
More tasteful than many of the
glass shops of Murano, the vases,
ornaments, dishes and other select
pieces of island glass here make
discriminating presents and souvenirs.

Emilia
Burano. Via San Mauro 296-303. The
largest lace shop on the island, selling
the widest choice: table linen, clothing,
handkerchiefs and other lacy garments
to suit all purses. Be prepared to pay a
lot for genuine Burano lace though.

Long Island
Lido. Viale Santa Maria Elisabetta 35.
Sportive swimwear for the Lido, in
case you forgot to pack your costume.

Mazzega
Murano. Ponte Vivarini 3. This
showroom, belonging to one of the big
names in glass manufacturing, has a
dazzling display of both ancient and
modern creations, from simple jugs
and glasses to the most elaborate
sculptures. There are also occasional
demonstrations of Venetian chandelier
production too.

141

Glass

The exact date when glass-making in Venice first began is unknown. The art, handed down from the Romans, was brought to the lagoon by travellers, but it had its decisive impetus during the Venetian heyday as a result of extensive contact with the East. Glass was made for some time in Venice before the Republic ordered the transfer of all factories to Murano in the late thirteenth century, as they were such a fire risk to the city.

It soon became the largest source of employment and income for the growing number of Muranese. The quality of their work, the originality of the designs and the perfection of their various techniques captured the world's attention, and for centuries Venetian glass had no rivals. The craftsmen were held in such high esteem that it was permissible for a Venetian nobleman to marry a glass-blower's daughter.

The oldest surviving examples of Murano glass date from the fourteenth century – chunky goblets of ruby red, indigo blue and emerald green, painted in enamel with scenes of weddings and other celebrations.

" *The mouths of the furnaces burn with a light almost as bright as the sun ... A rod is dipped in the red-hot paste ... a simple movement immediately gives it an embryo of shape, a blow of breath swells it ... and all around, incandescent blobs of glass stretch and smell like red balloons at a funfair.* "

Giovanni Comisso,
La Favorita

143

Towards the end of the fifteenth century, **transparent glass** was first produced. It was believed that these fine crystal drinking glasses would break into shivers if poison were put into them. After the introduction of crystal, other techniques were developed, including diamond engraving, gold leaf application, frosting, milk glass and fine filigree glass. Over the centuries, glassware followed architectural trends: in the wake of the baroque, it became highly curvaceous and ornamental; in response to the art nouveau movement, lines became simple and angular.

Today, despite the inevitable industrialisation of glass and the production of cheap glass frippery for the tourist market, old techniques and new artistic trends are still combined by the traditional manufacturing families of Murano. **Glass treasures** can still be found, and it remains a spell-binding sight to see a master glassmaker at work.

Excursions

La Serenissima's terra firma *empire* once stretched from the Adriatic to Lake Garda, and from the fertile plain of the Po to the foothills of the majestic, craggy Dolomite Mountains. Its spectacular, unspoilt countryside still resembles a Renaissance landscape painting.

145

Dolomiti

*On a clear day, the craggy, white, snow-tipped peaks of the mighty Dolomite Mountains are clearly visible from Venice. Named after the French geologist and mineralogist **Déodat Dolomieu** (1750–1801), and dominating the northern Veneto region, with their jagged, saw-edged ridges, deep gorges, colourful alpine meadows and icy, crystal-clear lakes, it is easy to see why so many consider the majestic Dolomites the most beautiful part of the Alps, especially at sunset and dawn, when bathed in a magical pink light.*

The Dolomites begin 80km (50 miles) north of Venice and are **Italy's last great wilderness region**, with coniferous forests cloaking the mountains, giving way to verdant alpine meadows and scree slopes above the tree level, fringing the permanent snow fields and glaciers which cloak the highest peaks. The area offers endless scope for walkers, climbers and winter sports enthusiasts, attracting visitors all year round. Even non-climbers can reach the heights and enjoy the far-reaching views, thanks to the extensive network of ski-lifts and cable cars.

The area is a veritable **paradise for nature lovers**, and supports an astonishing variety of wildlife. Look out in particular for gentians, edelweiss and alpine snow-bells on the flower-spangled upland meadows – home to marmots,

choughs and chamois. You may also see rock thrushes and alpine accentors on the scree slopes, while eagles circle overhead. Deer, hare, red squirrels, tree-creepers and woodpeckers can also be found on the wooded lower slopes.

Historic towns

The Dolomites are scattered with charming villages and towns, many with Tyrolean-style chalet houses and onion-domed churches – a legacy of Austro-Hungarian rule. In the unspoilt foothills, elegant **Asolo** is a popular port of call, as is **Bassano del Grappa**, famous for its fiery local spirit (*grappa*), its ceramics, its ancient wooden bridge and an annual asparagus festival (late April/early May). Scenic **Belluno**, at the confluence of two mountain rivers, with its arcaded Renaissance houses and impressive cathedral, is the gateway to the spectacular **Cadore valley**, and the birthplace of **Titian** is at picturesque **Pieve di Cadore**, an ideal base for exploring the **Bosco di Cansiglio**, a beautiful area of thick forests, lakes and hills. The trees from here provided much of the wood used in the construction of Venice. They were transported by raft down the Piave river to the lagoon.

Ski resorts

From October to March, snow cloaks the mountains, and the entire area becomes a massive winter playground boasting the premier ski resorts of Italy and some of the best, most snow-sure skiing in the Alps. The ski resorts of the Dolomites range from flatteringly easy one-run wonders to some of the most extensive domains in the world.

The most fashionable resort – **Cortina d'Ampezzo**, at the eastern end of the Strada delle Dolomite – first leapt to fame as host to the 1956 Winter Olympics. Today it is the 'St Moritz of Italy', a picturesque town, popular with rich Italians (many of whom have second homes here) who enjoy the chic shopping, the scenery, the lunching and the partying as much as the skiing. Picture-postcard **Madonna di Campiglio** is especially popular with intermediates and beginners. Lesser-known resorts include **Canazei**, **Campitello** and **Arabba**, which links up to the vast Dolomiti Superski circuits of **Selva** and **Sella Ronda**, with over 1 000km (620 miles) of piste. It is possible to ski all year round on **Marmolada**, at 3 343m (10 968ft) the highest peak in the Dolomites.

Lago di Garda

Lying in a deeply gouged valley between the regions of Veneto and Lombardy, Lake Garda is the largest of the northern lakes and a popular summer playground, set in beautiful countryside near the snow-capped peaks of the Dolomites. A string of attractive small towns and villages with peaches-and-cream houses dot its banks, and offer holidaymakers such facilities as luxury hotels with lakeside gardens, sophisticated shopping and dining, sandy beaches (albeit artificial), tennis, cycling, horse-riding, and a host of water-sports activities.

The climate is extraordinarily mild. However, the lake is seldom calm as there is usually a welcome breeze, which cools the blistering summer sun and makes Lake Garda, 140km (87 miles) west of Venice, a popular destination for wind-surfing and sailing. **Torbole** and **Riva del Garda**, two towns at the northern end of the lake, frequently host major international sailing events. Here the lake is narrow and fjord-like, hemmed in by sheer rock faces to the north and west and the 80km (50-mile) limestone ridge of **Monte**

Baldo to the east. The contrasting southern end of the lake, from **Gargnano** to **Salò**, opens out to form a beautiful and fertile coastal strip known as the **Riviera Bresciana**, with luxuriant vegetation and attractive lakeside promenades flanked by olives, palms and magnolias. Here in the south are some of the gems of Garda, including the villages of **Sirmione** and **Bardolino**.

Although the lake is 52km (32 miles) long and, at its broadest point, 16 1/2 km (10 1/4 miles) wide, it is easy to explore the lake and shore by ferry, with daily links between the various villages and towns. A trip from one end of the lake to the other takes about two and a half hours; there is a faster hydrofoil service around the lake, and excursion boats operate around the southern end. Alternatively, the 143km (89-mile) perimeter road, **La Gardesana**, is a sensational driving experience: it hugs the shores of the lake, frequently cutting through tunnels of solid rock or clinging to the narrow ledges of cliff faces, with numerous breathtaking *bella vistas* en route.

Each lakeside town has its own charm and attractions, but favourites include **Salò** – the birthplace of Gaspare da Salò, the inventor of the violin – an elegant pastel-coloured town on Garda's western shore with grand hotels and luxurious villas set in semi-tropical gardens along a long narrow bay; **Torbole**, a picturesque fishing village with smart shopping and excellent fish restaurants at the north-eastern corner of the lake; **Malcesiné** (on the eastern shore), where you can take a cable car to the summit of **Monte Baldo** for sensational views (especially at sunset); the nearby fishing village of **Bardolino**, which gives its name to the well-known red wine produced on the shores of the lake; **Riva del Garda** in the north and **Desenzano** in the south – two major resorts with a lively atmosphere and excellent nightlife; and **Sirmione**, a finger of land extending into the southern end of Lake Garda, connected to the mainland by a bridge.

Guarding the entrance to picturesque, pedestrianised Sirmione stands an imposing **medieval castle**, cleverly designed by the powerful Veronese Scaligeri family with an inner harbour to trap shipborne invaders. The Roman poet **Catullus** owned a villa here in the ninth century BC. A delightful lakeside walk along the eastern shore links the village to the **Grotte di Catullo** ruins amid ancient olive trees at the northern tip of the peninsula.

Padua

Padua is the nearest large town to Venice, just a 30-minute train-ride away. A flourishing university town since the Middle Ages, today Padua is a wealthy city with a population of a quarter of a million. During World War Two it suffered extensive damage, but the bulk of the medieval centre escaped the bombing, as did the city's two greatest treasures: the Cappella degli Scrovegni, containing one of Italy's foremost fresco cycles, and the Basilica di Sant' Antonio, one of the country's most celebrated religious shrines with some of the Veneto's finest sculptures. The rest of the city contains a handful of sights easily viewed on foot in a day trip from Venice.

Basilica di Sant' Antonio

Piazza del Santo. Tel: 049 8242811. Open: Oct–Mar, daily 0630–2000; Nov–Feb, daily 0630–1900.

The monumental multi-domed Basilica of St Anthony, locally known as Il Santo, was built in the fourteenth century to house the body of St Anthony, the patron saint of Padua, renowned for his humility and gentleness and his devotion to the poor. Streams of devotees attend the Cappella dell'Arca in the north transept to pay their respects at his tomb, to touch and kiss its polished stone, or to leave votive offerings – anything from photographs of missing children to mementos of people who have survived car crashes thanks to his assistance. The surrounding walls are adorned with marble reliefs depicting scenes from his life by Sansovino and Lombardi. The high altar has a magnificent series of St Anthony reliefs by Donatello together with bronze statues of the crucifixion, the Virgin and various Paduan saints.

In the piazza outside the church stands Donatello's famous equestrian statue of *Gattamelata*. Dated 1447, it was the first bronze statue of size produced in Italy since Roman times. It shows the great *condottiere* (military leader) **Erasmo da Narni**, whose smooth-talking diplomatic skills earned him the nickname 'Gattamelata' – the 'honeyed cat'.

Cappella degli Scrovegni

Part of the Museo Civico Eremitani (see below). Piazza Eremitani 8. Tel: 049 8204550. Open: Tue–Sun 0900–1800. £££ (including entry to the Museo Civico Eremitani).

Paduan nobleman **Enrico Scrovegni** built this small chapel to atone for the usurious sins of his father, condemned to eternal damnation by **Dante** in his *Inferno*. He commissioned **Giotto** to decorate it between 1303 and 1305, and the resulting fresco cycle is among the greatest achievements in the history of art. The sense of pictorial space, naturalism and narrative drama marked a decisive break with the Byzantine tradition of the preceding 1 000 years, and the start of the modern era in painting.

The chapel is bathed in a cool blue light which creates an air of calm for you to admire the *Story of Mary and Jesus*, portrayed in 38 square panels on the altar and both side walls, connected within a group of geometric marble designs, with episodes from the Old Testament and busts of saints and prophets. The brilliant colours are imbued with light, the blues, reds and golds in particular giving life to the figures and animating the landscapes. The entire west wall of the chapel is taken up with a formal presentation of *The Last Judgement,* its style closer to Byzantine tradition than some of the other frescos, with parts probably painted by assistants. Immediately above the door, one scene depicts Scrovegni offering a model of the chapel to the Virgin.

151

Central Padua

*Especially attractive for a stroll is the tightly knit medieval heart of the town, with its narrow arcaded streets, ancient town hall and surrounding squares. In sunny, café-lined Piazza Cavour you will find the legendary **Caffè Pedrocchi**, a monumental neo-classical edifice (rebuilt after World War Two) which, when it first opened in 1831, was the largest café in Europe, open 24 hours a day. It remains the place to see and be seen in when going for a coffee in Padua.*

Nearby, the medieval **Palazzo Municipale** (town hall) is disguised behind a contemporary façade. Opposite is the main university building, its colonnaded courtyard decorated with the family crests of distinguished rectors and graduates. Heading westwards, lively **Piazza delle Frutta** and **Piazza delle Erbe** are always ablaze with colour, thanks to their daily fruit and vegetable markets. In between, the **Palazzo della Ragione** ('Palace of Reason') was Padua's medieval law court (*tel: 049 8205006; open: Tue–Sun 0900–1800; £*). Its interior contains 333 fascinating frescos on an astrological theme.

Further west still, and bounded by charming arcades, **Piazza dei Signori** contains the **Loggia del Consiglio**, an elegant Renaissance building which once housed the ruling body of the city, and the **Palazzo del Capitanio**, with its handsome clock tower, which was formerly the seat of the Venetian governor. Continue a short distance to the southwest, to visit the **Duomo** (*Piazza del Duomo; tel: 049 662814; open: daily 0730–1200, 1545–1930*), the city's airy, bright and unadorned cathedral. Next door, the interior of the tiny brick-built **Baptistery** (*Piazza del Duomo, tel: 049 656914; open: daily 0730–1300, 1500–1800; £*) is smothered in the most beautiful fourteenth-century frescos.

Musei Civici Eremitani

Piazza Eremitani 8. Tel: 049 8204550. Open: Tue–Sun 0900–1800. £££ (includes entry to the Scrovegni Chapel).

Padua's civic museum complex is housed within the fourteenth-century cloisters adjoining the medieval church of the Eremitani, a reclusive Augustinian order. Highlights include the **Archaeological Museum** and the second-floor **Gallery**, with an impressive collection of paintings of the Veneto. The **Bottacin Museum** of coins and medals is also contained here, and the **Scrovegni Chapel** (*see page 151*), which stands on the same site, overlooking the remains of a Roman amphitheatre.

Prato della Valle

This piazza, nicknamed the Prato ('field'), claims to be the largest public square in Italy. Its oval shape reflects the form of the Roman theatre that stood there, and today, following major restoration, it has been returned to its Renaissance glory, encircled by a newly dredged canal and **78 statues of celebrated Paduans**. Its verdant lawns and gently trickling water make it an enjoyable place to pause awhile in summer.

Brenta Canal

Times and fares of these trips are available from hotel concierges, travel agents and tourist information offices. The boats usually depart from San Marco around 0900 and arrive in Padua at approximately 1800, with the return journey made by bus or train. Advance booking is essential.

One of the most popular excursions from Venice is a boat trip to Padua (in summer months only) along the Brenta Canal. Some 80 Renaissance villas, built as summer retreats for Venetian patricians, scatter the countryside, and the excursion enables visitors to stop at several en route, including **Villa Foscari** (also known as La Malcontenta), one of the great Paduan architect **Andrea Palladio**'s best-known and most beautiful creations (*see pages 162–3*).

153

Verona I

*After Venice, Verona is the second largest city in the Veneto region and one of the most prosperous in northern Italy, a bustling commercial city also rich in history, art and architecture. Located 120km (75 miles) west of **Venice**, it is best known as the setting of Shakespeare's **Romeo and Juliet**, and for its Roman remains, notably a magnificent amphitheatre – the venue of a world-famous opera festival.*

For much of its history, Verona was dominated by other cities and rulers. The prehistoric settlement of Verona became a Roman colony in 89 BC, and soon developed into a town of considerable importance, as the size and grandeur of its classical remains testify. Later, Charlemagne's son **Pepin** ruled here as King of Italy, then the Saxon and Hohenstaufen emperors found it a convenient base from which to control Italy. It was controlled until 1797 by the Venetian Republic, then it was the turn of France, then Austria. Finally, in 1866 Verona joined the newly united kingdom of Italy, thereby ending centuries of 'foreign' rule.

Thankfully, the vibrant, provincial city of today has survived its chequered history with most of its Roman, medieval and Renaissance monuments intact. Contained within massive sixteenth-century walls, and clustered around the swift Adige river, the picturesque streets and squares of its compact historic core are still laid out according to the grid pattern decreed by **Emperor Augustus**, and many of its ancient *palazzi* stand on Roman foundations. Even some of the more modern buildings have little bits of Roman marblework embedded in their façades. The centre is largely pedestrianised, and most of the sights are within easy walking distance of each other.

The Arena

Piazza Bra. Tel: 045 8003204. Open: Tue–Sun 0800–1900 (0815–1500 during the opera season in July and August). ££.

Verona's massive amphitheatre is the third largest in the world (after Rome's **Colosseum** and the arena at **Capua**, near Naples), and the interior has miraculously survived virtually intact. Built around AD 30 with seating for 14 000, in its heyday it could hold the entire population of Roman Verona and visitors would flock from the far corners of the Veneto to watch its bloody contests: combats to the death between men and wild beasts, or between pairs of gladiators, butchering one another to the cries of '*Jugula!*' ('Slit his throat!').

From the **44 tiers** of the arena, you can see the maze of dungeons and underground passages where the animals were kept in cages, then winched up to arena level. The word *arena* is Latin for 'sand'; after their slaughter, attendants dressed as Charon (the mythical ferryman of the dead) would carry off the bodies and rake sand over the blood, ready for the next bout.

Nowadays, the arena is used for theatre performances, pop concerts and dazzling opera performances (*see page 161*).

Castelvecchio

Corso Castelvecchio 2. Tel: 045 594734. Open: Tue–Sun 0900–1830. ££.

This graceful castle was once the former home of the **Scaligeri family**, one-time powerful medieval rulers of Verona, and is now the **Museo Civico d'Arte**, one of the finest galleries in the Veneto. Its maze of courtyards, chambers and an overhead walkway affords sensational views of Verona and the surrounding countryside, which are almost as appealing as the superb displays of art and artefacts inside. These include important canvases by **Mantegna**, **Giovanni Bellini**, **Veronese**, **Tintoretto**, **Tiepolo** and **Canaletto**, together with an extensive collection by local artists.

Verona II

Casa di Giulietta

Via Cappello 23. Tel: 045 8034303. Open: Tue–Sun 0800–1900. ££.

The **House of Juliet** certainly looks the part with its quaint marble balcony and romantic courtyard setting at the heart of the old town, but there is no evidence linking this house with the **Romeo and Juliet legend**. As Arnold Bennett once observed: 'The balcony is too high for love!'

> " *There is no world without Verona's walls,*
> *But purgatory, torture, hell itself.*
> *Hence – banished is banish'd from the world –*
> *And world's exile is death …* "
>
> **William Shakespeare, *Romeo and Juliet*, 1594**

Even so, it doesn't seem to put off the half a million visitors who come each year, lured by the romance of the story, and eager to have their picture taken on Juliet's balcony or outside the beautiful red-brick Gothic **Casa di Romeo** in nearby Via delle Arche Scaligeri.

Even if these attractions are fakes, the **Montagu** and **Capulet** families did indeed exist, not constantly feuding but living amicably in their respective castles near Vicenza. The first person to write the story of the star-crossed lovers was a Vicentine noble, **Luigi da Porto**, in 1530. It was not until four centuries later, with the advent of mass tourism, that Verona started to exploit the Romeo and Juliet myth, and today the House of Juliet remains one of the most popular sights in the city.

Churches

Verona is blessed with more than its fair share of beautiful churches. The largest – **Sant' Anastasia**, on the river – contains some striking frescos, including **Pisanello's *St George*** in the sacristy and faded fifteenth-century scenes from the life of St Peter in the Gothic portal. Nearby, the **Duomo** (cathedral) is known for its exterior carvings, the richly decorated altars of its magnificent interior, Romanesque cloisters and **Titian's *Assumption*** (in the first chapel on the left).

The beautiful **San Zeno Maggiore**, built between 1123 and 1135 to house the relics of Verona's patron saint, is northern Italy's most ornate Romanesque church, with a magnificent ship's-keel ceiling, an intricately carved marble façade and an altarpiece by **Mantegna**.

Tiny **Santa Maria Antica**, also Romanesque, is dominated by the **Scaligeri tombs**. As it was their parish church, this famous Veronese family chose to be buried here, and their graves are marked by elaborate Gothic tombs depicting them as soldiers – a permanent reminder of their military prowess.

Across the river, **Santo Stefano** is among the city's oldest churches, and **San Giorgio in Braida** is a fine example of a domed Renaissance church – a rare sight in Verona. Inside, it contains Veronese's spectacular altarpiece *The Martyrdom of St George*.

Piazza delle Erbe

The elongated main square of the old town is among the most lovely in all Italy, situated on the site of the old Roman forum. Named Piazza delle Erbe after the city's ancient herb market, it is now a colourful fruit and vegetable market. The **Lion**

of St Mark atop the marble column at the northern end of the square is the symbol of Venetian authority (Verona was the principal city of La Serenissima's *terra firma* empire from 1405 until 1797). The fountain in the middle of the square is often overlooked by eager buyers at the market stalls, yet its Madonna statue dates from Roman times.

157

The market is an ideal place to purchase mouth-watering picnic fare to enjoy in the scenic countryside surrounding Verona, and there is also a tempting assortment of cafés, restaurants and shops around the square.

Vicenza

Wealthy Vicenza, the capital of the Veneto, is an elegant historic town 50km (31 miles) west of Venice straddling the River Bacchiglione, on the edge of the fertile Po plain. Here, Andrea Palladio, the most influential of Italian architects, spent much of his life, and you can see here his beautifully preserved theatre, basilica and several of his palaces – one of which (Palazzo Chiericati) houses the fascinating civic museum and gallery. On a hill just outside the city, La Rotonda (see page 163) is the most famous of all Palladian villas.

Corso Palladio

Vicenza's main street provides a clear impression of the city's wealth and beauty, lined by handsome Palladian palaces including **Palazzo Bonin** (at No 13), **Palazzo Zilere dal Verme** (at No 42) and **Palazzo da Schio** (at No 147) – also known as Ca' d'Oro owing to its resemblance to Venice's once gilt-swathed 'House of Gold' (*see page 24*). Many of Vicenza's smartest shops and cafés are to be found in **Corso Palladio**, under the arcades.

Palazzo Chiericati (Museo Civico)

Piazza Matteotti 37-39. Tel: 0444 321384. Open: Apr–Sept, Tue–Sun 1000–1900; Oct–Mar, Tue–Sun 0900–1700. £££ (combined entry with the Teatro Olimpico and Museo Naturale e Archeologico).

Vicenza's Civic Museum is housed in one of Palladio's finest town houses. On the ground floor are interesting local archaeological collections. But the museum's real appeal is the **impressive picture gallery** on the first floor, which contains major works by local painters (including **Montagna** and **Buonconsiglio**), alongside such familiar names as **Tintoretto**, **Tiepolo**, **Van Dyck** and **Bellini**.

Piazza dei Signori

Palladio's presence is felt once again in Vicenza's lively main square: the massive, green-roofed Renaissance town hall – now called the **Basilica Palladiana** (*open: Tue–Sun 0900–1700*) – was his first major triumph, with its revolutionary design that encased the original Gothic *palazzo* within a two-storey loggia. The square is surrounded by grand fifteenth-century residences constructed for Vicenza's wealthy citizens, the slender-brick **Torre di Piazza** (82m (269ft) high) and a variety of shops and cafés. At the western end of the basilica is a **marble statue of Palladio**, usually surrounded by market stalls overflowing from Piazza delle Erbe. At the northwest corner of Piazza dei Signori, the **Loggia del Capitanio** (formerly the residence of the Venetian governor) was begun by Palladio in 1571 and decorated with victorious scenes from the Battle of Lepanto.

Teatro Olimpico

Piazza Matteotti 11. Tel: 0444 323781. Open: Apr–Sept, Tue–Sun 1000–1900; Oct–Mar, Tue–Sun 0900–1700. £££ (combined entry with the Museo Civico and Museo Naturale e Archeologico).

Opposite Palazzo Chiericati, the Teatro Olimpico is Palladio's last work, begun in 1580 and completed by **Scamozzi** five years later. Built of wood and stucco, this remarkable building is a Renaissance adaptation of the classical style of amphitheatre, and the **earliest surviving indoor theatre** of modern times. The auditorium, with seating for 1 000, rises in steep, semi-circular wooden tiers, with an elaborate balustrade surmounted by ancient statues. The permanent stage-set, with its three openings and *trompe-l'œil* street scenes evoking Renaissance Vicenza, were cleverly painted in exaggerated perspective to give the illusion of great depth. The set was created by Scamozzi for the theatre's first production (and for many years its only one) of Sophocles' **Oedipus Rex** in 1585. The play was commissioned by the **Accademia Olimpica**, a learned society of local humanists (including Palladio, a founding member) which still exists today.

159

Cafés and restaurants

Al Bersagliere
Padua. Via Donatello 6. Tel: 049 8760314. £££. Closed: Wed. This small, rustic *trattoria* near the Prato serves traditional Paduan cuisine and a good selection of regional wines.

Le Pen
Padua. Piazza Cavour 15. Tel: 049 8759483. ££. Closed: Sun. A popular pizzeria with a wide choice of dishes, including fish-based pizzas.

Olivo
Verona. Piazza Bra 18. Tel: 045 8030598. ££. Closed: Mon, and Tue lunchtime. Sophisticated pizzeria overlooking the Arena, with smart, modern décor.

Pampanin
Verona. Via Garibaldi 24. £. Open: Wed–Mon 0730–0000, except Aug. This riverside *gelateria* serves Verona's finest ice-cream.

Pizza & Café
Verona. Via Scala 2. £. A trendy café, popular with a young crowd for coffee, snacks and beers.

Antica Casa della Malvasia
Vicenza. Contrà Morette 5. Tel: 0444 543704. ££. Closed: Sun evening, Mon and Aug. Hearty home-cooking in an ancient Veneto inn, with live music (jazz/blues) most Tuesday evenings.

Tre Visi
Vicenza. Corso Palladio 25. Tel: 0444 324868. ££. Closed: Sun evening and Mon. A popular locals' haunt, serving traditional Vicentine dishes in a quiet courtyard near the historic town centre.

Vino from the Veneto

The Veneto produces large quantities of red, white and rosé wines, with white the most popular with locals. Soave is the main 'big-name' white wine of the region, although the best-quality whites actually come from Friuli and Trentino-Alto Adige regions. If you get the chance, try Bianco di Custoza, an 'upmarket' Soave from the eastern shores of Lake Garda, and sweet Gambellara (made with Soave grapes), an exceptional white dessert wine. Popular light, fruity reds include Bardolino, also from Lake Garda, and Valpolicella, while rich Recioto della Valpolicella and fortified Recioto Amarone count among the best red dessert wines.

Shopping

Every town in the Veneto boasts an excellent range of food shops, and many have seasonal speciality markets. In country areas you can buy wines, cheese and olive oil direct from the producers. Verona is also strong on fashion with Max Mara, Versace, Stefanel, Benetton, Gucci and Fiorucci, among others, in the main shopping street (Via Mazzini) alone.

Rinascente
Padua. Piazza Garibaldi. Smart, affordable fashions and stylish household goods in a popular, national department store.

Les Bonbons
Verona. Via Garibaldi 12a. A tiny, old-fashioned sweet shop, chock-a-block with gorgeous sweets and chocolates.

Città' del Sole
Verona. Via Cattaneo 8b. Dreams are made of this! A toyshop selling everything imaginable, from dolls to dinosaurs and dumper trucks.

Al Duca d'Aosta
Verona. Via Mazzini 31. Chic local women and men's fashions, made in Mestre.

Gulliver
Verona. Via Stella 16b. A small specialist travel bookshop with a staggering number of guides, maps, videos and literature, in various languages.

Patrizia Fontana
Vicenza. Palazzo Terzi, Corso Fogazzaro 94. Pamper yourself with treats from this luxurious bathroom accessory shop.

Pianeta Loriet
Vicenza. Galleria Porti 3. Designer separates for men and women by Montana, Gianfranco Ferre, CK, Dolce & Gabbana and Versus.

Stecco
Vicenza. Piazza dei Signori 57. Jewellery made in Vicenza, the 'city of gold' – one of the main Italian centres for the working of this precious metal.

Nightlife

The two main cultural venues in the Veneto hinterland are Verona's **Arena** (staging everything from a spectacular summer opera festival to pop concerts) and the **Teatro Olimpico** in Vicenza. Tickets for Arena events are available from the official box office (*Via Dietro Anfiteatro 6b; tel: 045 8005151; open: Mon–Fri 0900–1200, 1515–1745; Sat 0900–1200 during the festival, 1000– 2100 on performance days, 1000– 1745 on days without performances; or book online at www.arena.it*). For details of the Teatro Olimpico's theatre season, contact the Vicenza tourist office (*Piazza Duomo 5; tel: 0444 544122*).

Palladio

A recurring theme throughout the Veneto is the genius of Andrea Palladio (1508–80). Born in Padua, he moved to Vicenza at the age of 16 to work in a stone-carving workshop. While working on the decorative details of a new villa here, he met powerful local aristocrat Count Trissino, *the leader of a group of humanist intellectuals dedicated to the revival of classical culture. Impressed by the young stone-cutter, Trissino agreed to fund his studies of ancient architecture, and even financed several research trips to Rome.*

As a result, Palladio developed a new, unique architectural style by reinventing such classical features as **porticos**, **arcades**, **domes** and **pedimented pavilions** – all hallmarks of his designs. His early patrons were mainly Vicentine nobles, for whom he designed country villas, and Venetian patricians, keen to acquire a newly fashionable estate on the mainland.

Palladio's first major break came in 1549 when his ingenious design for Vicenza's Gothic town hall (now called the **Basilica Palladiana**; *see page 159*) established him as the leading Italian architect of his day. From here to his last great triumph, the **Teatro Olimpico** (*see page 159*), he totally transformed the appearance of Vicenza – a city still celebrated the world over for its architecture.

Each of his designs, although always unmistakably 'Palladian', is surprisingly different, ranging from the ornate, statue-clad **Palazzo Chiericati** in Vicenza (*see pages 158–9*) to the simple, unadorned **Villa Pisani Ferri** at Bagnolo di Lonigo. Palladio ideally liked to build near water, and would create classical gardens for each villa, believing the natural

environment was vital to 'help conserve the health and
strength of the villa's inhabitants, and restore their spirits,
worn out by the agitation of city life, to peace and tranquillity'
(*Quattro Libri dell'Architettura*, 1570).

Villa Rotonda near Vicenza – a dazzling white edifice,
striking for its regular, symmetrical forms, its simple design
and pleasing proportions, balanced by neat green lawns
and terracotta roof tiles – is widely considered his greatest
achievement. It has since inspired lookalikes as far afield as
London, Delhi and St Petersburg. With Palladian designs
continuing to influence architects around the world, perhaps
it should come as no surprise that Palladio is considered the
most influential architect of all time.

Lifestyles
Shopping, eating, children and nightlife in Venice

Shopping

Since its heyday in the Middle Ages, when it was a leading trading centre between the East and West, Venice has been a dream destination for shopping. Centuries on, the hundreds of specialist shops that line its charming calli *and* campi *are a constant draw for visitors. A strong artisan tradition remains, with **marbled paper**, **Murano glass** and **carnival masks** the most popular souvenirs. Venice has the additional advantage of being totally pedestrianised, and, with shops scattered across the city, shopping can easily be combined with sightseeing.*

Where to shop

Venice's main shopping areas are the **Mercerie** – a series of jam-packed, narrow alleyways stretching from the Rialto to St Mark's Square – and the labyrinth of streets to the immediate north and west of St Mark's collectively known as the **Frezzeria**. The **Strada Nova in**

Cannaregio is also one of the busiest shopping streets, especially good for foodstuffs and affordable fashions.

On the opposite side of the Grand Canal, the greatest density of shops is centred on the Rialto area. **Calle Ruga Vecchia di San Giovanni** in particular has excellent pasta, cheese and salami stores and a host of

fashion boutiques, leatherware and craft shops. Prices are lower here than in the smarter Mercerie and the Frezzeria zone. The Venetian maze is full of hidden treasures, so it is especially rewarding to leave the main streets and explore the lesser-known back alleys, rich in local stores, galleries, antiquarians and craft workshops.

Fabrics and lace

The paintings and palace furnishings of ancient Venice bear witness to the city's long tradition of richly coloured and textured fabrics. Even the name 'Mercerie' means 'haberdashers', described by John Evelyn in 1645 as 'one of the most delicious streets in the world' because of its abundant textile shops. **Bevilacqua** (*Ponte della Canonica 337b, San Marco*) has been making its sumptuous velvets and luxurious brocades on hand looms since 1875, but the city's best-known fabric outlet is **Trois** (*Campo San Maurizio 2665, San Marco*), a tiny shop specialising in

fabrics by famous couturier **Mariano Fortuny**, the son of a Catalan artist and fabric-collector who moved to make his fortune in Venice in 1889, renowned especially for his fine pleated silk dresses that could be rolled up and threaded through a wedding ring.

Your best bet for Venetian lace, though, is the island of Burano (*see pages 132–3*), but for reliable, top-quality lace in Venice itself, try **Jesurum** (*Merceria del Capitello 4857, San Marco*) or **Annelie** (*Calle Lunga San Barnaba 2748, Dorsoduro*).

Fashion

Most of the big names in Italian fashion can be found within a stone's throw of St Mark's Square. The smartest shopping streets in town are the elegant Via Larga XXII Marzo (**Laura Biagiotti**, **Bruno Magli** and **Bulgari**), and the adjoining glitzy Salizzada San Moisè (**Valentino**, **Prada** and **Versace**).

The Mercerie, between St Mark's and the Rialto, is most popular for tourist shopping sprees, combining further designer outlets with such high-street boutiques as **Benetton** and **Max & Co** (the 'cheaper' version of **Max Mara**). Venetians favour **Coin** (*Salizzada San Giovanni Crisostomo 5787, Cannaregio*), the city's main department store, for reasonably priced, stylish clothing for men and women, while cheaper, more 'with-it' fashions can be found near the Rialto and along Strada Nova.

You will be spoilt for choice in terms of Italian leatherware. For elegant, expensive shoes you can't beat **Fendi** (*Salizzada San Moisè 1474, San Marco*) or **Bottega Veneta** (*Calle Vallaresso 1337, San Marco*), with its trendy designs made in Vicenza. The greatest Venetian name for bags, belts and wallets is **Vogini** (*Calle Ascensione 1257, San Marco*) near St Mark's Square. Many tourists, however, settle for the ersatz **Prada**, **Vuitton** and **Chanel** bags and belts touted by street sellers on Calle Larga XXII Marzo and Riva degli Schiavoni.

Glass

Considering the Venetians have always had such good taste in art and architecture, they have created a surprising amount of vulgar glass frippery, from dinky glass animals to gondola lamp-stands. However, it is still possible to find truly beautiful pieces, made with a purity of design and strong Venetian character (*see pages 142–3*). For the best buys, focus your attention on the most respected glass-makers on Murano island, such as **Barovier e Tosso** (*Fondamenta Vetrai 28, Murano*) and **Salviati** (*Fondamenta Radi 16, Murano*). In Venice, the best-known glass shops are in and around St Mark's Square, but be prepared to dig deep into your pockets!

Masks

The recent revival of the carnival has resulted in nearly as many mask shops as glass shops in Venice. Many are cheap and mass-produced, but a genuine leather or *papier-mâché* mask makes a marvellous souvenir. At some shops, including **Ca' Macana** (*Calle dei Botteghe 3172, Dorsoduro*), you can watch the masks being made. Before purchasing one, find out whether it is a *fantasia* ('fantasy mask') or a character from the

Commedia dell'Arte. Miniature china masks are also attractive collectors' items.

Paper

The ancient Italian craft of marbled paper manufacture is still a thriving industry in Venice. The elegant hand-made writing paper, notebooks, photo albums and photo frames sold in the city's many *legatoria* ('book-binders') make lovely gifts. **Legatoria Piazzese** (*Campiello della Feltrina 2511c, San Marco*) is the last remaining paper-maker to use old hand- and woodblock printing techniques, while the workshop of **Alberto Valese-Ebru** (*Campiello San Stefano 3471, San Marco*) produces some of the city's most innovative designs.

Markets

The city's most colourful shopping attraction is the **Erberia**, Venice's fruit and vegetable market in San Polo overlooking the Grand Canal near the Rialto Bridge, and the **Pescheria** (fish market), set in an arcaded neo-Gothic hall by the quayside (*see page 54*). There is also a daily general market along **Rio Terra San Leonardo in Cannaregio** in summer, and the occasional stalls along the **Strada Nova** selling silk scarves, ties and leather goods.

Antique shops dot the city, with the greatest concentration around **Campo San Maurizio** where twice a year, in the week before Easter and Christmas, there is an **antiques market**. In summer months, souvenir-hunters will delight in the stalls which clutter the **Riva degli Schiavoni**, with their vast array of trinkets ranging from gondolier hats to Venice 'snow storms'.

Opening hours

Major shops are generally open Monday to Saturday from 0800 or 0900 to 1930, although many tourist shops maintain longer hours. Most smaller shops also take a long lunch break from 1230 or 1300 to 1530 or 1600. Many shops (except grocers) are closed on Monday mornings. Food stores tend to close on Wednesday afternoons, and virtually everything shuts on Sundays, except at peak season when many stay open all day Sunday too. English is spoken in most shops, and credit cards are accepted in most places.

169

Eating out

Venetian cuisine is simple and tasty, relying on the huge variety of fish and seafood found in the lagoon and the Adriatic, combined with the freshest of seasonal meats, cheeses and vegetables from the mainland, best accompanied by the wines of the Veneto, one of the top wine-growing regions of Italy.

What's in a name?

Venice boasts over 300 restaurants with a bewildering variety of names. Originally, a *ristorante* was marginally smarter than the more homely, simple *trattoria* or *osteria*, but nowadays there is little difference. The only distinction between them now is that some are modern and elegant, others are rustic and characterful; some overlook charming canals, others spill out on to sunny piazzas or cool, green courtyards.

As the names suggest, a *birreria* and a *spaghetteria* are cheap, cheerful eateries that sell beer, pasta dishes and snacks. Pizzas are not exactly local specialities but, as everywhere in Italy, you can find good-value **pizzerias**. The better ones use wood-ovens and tend to open only in the evenings. Many restaurants display a set-price *menu turistico* with a choice of a couple of dishes for each course, often rather run-of-the-mill and offering little opportunity to sample the delicious local cuisine. A better bet for those on a tight budget is to settle for a pasta dish and a salad (permitted in all but the smartest places), or a snack at a traditional *bacaro*.

A *bacaro* is a basic, old-fashioned and often boisterous bar where locals go at lunchtime or in the evening for an *ombra* – a small glass of white wine (*vino bianco*), unless you specify red (*rosso*). The name comes from the age-old habit of workers having a cool drink in the shade (*ombra*) at midday.

Most *bacari* serve snacks called *cicchetti* – the Venetian equivalent

salted cod mixed to a paste with olive oil, parsley and garlic) and *carpaccio*. This exquisite dish was devised in Venice by **Giuseppe Cipriani**, founder of Harry's Bar (*see page 106*) for the countess Amalia Mocenigo who, in order to keep slim, ate only raw tenderloin. At the time, there was a major exhibition on the great artist Carpaccio – hence the name.

The first course, or *Primo piatto*, is usually rice, pasta or soup. Typical Venetian dishes include *brodo di pesce* (fish soup), *bigoli in salsa* (pasta with anchovy sauce) and many different types of risotto: *risotto di mare* (with shellfish), *risotto alla sbirraglia* (with chicken, vegetables and ham), *risotto alla travigiana* (made with red chicory from Treviso) and *risi e bisi* (risotto with peas).

The *Secondo piatto* ('second course') comprises fish or meat, accompanied by vegetables (*contorni*) or salad (*insalata*), which are never included in the price of the main course. Some local specialities – *fegato alla Veneziana* (calves' liver with onion and polenta) and *seppie in nero* (squid in black ink) – are an acquired taste. Fish dishes predominate, and include grilled *gamberetti* (prawns), *anguilla in umido* (eels in a tomato and white wine sauce) and *sarde in saor* (sardines in a sweet and sour sauce), one of many ancient 'Venetian'

of Spanish tapas – offering an excellent opportunity to sample the taste of everyday Venice. Try the anchovies, artichoke hearts, mini pizzas (*pizzetas*), spicy meatballs (*polpete*) and tiny sandwiches (*tramezzini*) with a wide assortment of fillings. *Cicchetti e l'ombra* ('a snack in the shade') is a Venetian tradition, as is the *giro de l'ombra* – a Venetian pub crawl.

A fine line separates a *bacaro* from many *osterie* (inns), except in the latter you can have a snack at the bar or a choice of hot dishes at a table, and they usually have longer opening hours. This half-bar/half-restaurant arrangement provides a relaxed, informal atmosphere characteristic of so many authentic Venetian restaurants.

Deciphering the menu

A typical meal will commence with *antipasti* (hors d'oeuvres) – usually a dazzling selection of tasty titbits including such delights as *fiori di zucchini* (courgette flowers stuffed with fish mousse), Parma ham with fresh figs, *baccalà mantecata* (dried

171

specialities acquired from the courts of sheikhs and sultans during the city's trading heyday with the East.

For dessert (*dolce*), try the delectable *tiramisu* (a light, creamy chocolate, coffee, mascarpone and brandy pudding), the many flavoured ice-creams (*gelati*) and *biscotti* (tiny dessert biscuits dipped in sweet wine). Cheese lovers will enjoy such regional delights as *asiago*, *montasio* and *fontina*. Coffee always rounds off the meal, often with a *digestivo* (digestive liqueur) or some *amaretti* (small almond biscuits).

Local drinks

The Veneto is a prolific wine-growing area, producing the largest output in Italy of superior DOC (Denominazione di Origine Controllata) wines, and considerably more white than red. Big names include the light, fruity reds of **Bardolino** and **Valpolicella** and the cheap, cheerful white **Soave** wines. **Tocai** and **Cuxtoza** whites and the red **Cabernets** and **Merlots** are also highly recommended, and in

winter you can find some lesser-known sweetish wines, such as **Recioto**, **Ramandolo** or **Zibibbo**. Most can be tasted in the restaurants and *bacari*, but to sample a wide range visit an **enoteca** (specialist wine shop and bar).

Venice is also noted for its cocktails, especially the **Bellini** created in Harry's Bar (*see page 106*) and its variants: **Mimosa** (with orange juice) and **Tiziano** (with red grape juice). **Martini** and **Campari** are favourite aperitifs, together with the herbal **Punt e Mes** and **Cynar** (made from artichokes). Campari is frequently mixed with white wine and soda to make a refreshing spritzer. The Veneto's sparkling wine, *prosecco*, is a refreshing drink at any time of day, drunk either *secco* (dry), *amabile* (medium sweet), *frizzante* (semi-sparkling) or *spumante* (sparkling). The classic after-dinner liqueur is *grappa*, a colourless, fiery schnapps that comes from the Veneto.

Eating habits

Most locals eat lunch (*pranzo*) around 1230 and dinner (*cena*) from 2000, but many restaurants serve dinner earlier to cater for visitors. Italians tend to dress up for dinner, with smart casual clothes the general rule, and it is advisable always to **book a table**. Children are generally accepted in restaurants, although they rarely provide special facilities such as high chairs. Likewise, few restaurants make special provision for wheelchairs, and few set aside space for non-smokers.

Most restaurants post menus and price lists outside to avoid any unpleasant surprises when the bill (*il conto*) arrives. However, the cost of the meal will usually be marked up with a cover charge (*pane e coperto*) and a service charge (*servizio*) of between 10 per cent and 15 per cent. Tipping on top of this is a matter of discretion. Most restaurants will accept credit cards, but cash is preferred.

Venice with children

Considering how much Italians adore children, there is surprisingly little laid on specifically for them in Venice. However, with a little imagination, it can become a magical city for them, a giant adventure playground where even the simplest of daily activities are a thrill: feeding the pigeons, visiting mask shops, watching glass-blowers or canal dredgers in action, eating pizza and ice-cream, and counting bridges (there are 416 in total!).

Aquatic activities

The ultimate treat for children is a gondola ride, or a trip across the Grand Canal on a *traghetto* (gondola-ferry). Also, jumping on and off *vaporetti* is brilliant fun for most kids. One favourite route for children is route 82, a circular route from **Riva degli Schiavoni** across to **Giudecca**, past the big ships in the port area and down the **Grand Canal** back to the start.

The canals provide an endless source of entertainment, with their variety of water-craft: fireboats, ambulance-boats, even Coca-Cola and Findus fishfinger boats! Take them to the interlocking bridges at **Tre Ponte** (*see page 39*) to spot the other twelve bridges, all visible at the same time, and to the junction between **Ponte del Paradiso** and **Ponte dei Preti** (in Castello near Campo Santa Maria Formosa), where they can safely jump from one bridge to the other without touching the ground.

In fine weather, it is fun to visit the islands. Kids love watching the glass-blowers at work in their workshops in **Murano**, and afterwards need little encouragement to start collecting the cheap, small glass animals with their holiday spending money. The best destination, however, is undoubtedly the **Lido** (*see page 135*) – an ideal venue for a family holiday with its sandy beaches, tennis, cycling and horse-riding facilities.

Parks

Most Venetian children can be found playing in local squares. However, there is a small, dusty playground with swings and slides in the **Giardini Pubblici**, the city's main park, which is also a good spot for a picnic. There is a grassy play area

and a roller-blading rink at **Sant' Elena**, in eastern Castello. Teenagers may also like to come here to see Venezia (Venice's football team) play at their home ground (*tel: 041 985100 for ticket information*).

Museums

Most Venetian museums are decidedly 'hands-off'. However, for older children there is much to entertain them in the **Naval History Museum** (*see page 118*) with its model ships and guns, the eccentric artworks and gardens of the **Collezione Guggenheim** (*see pages 74–5*), and the reproduction pharmacy and puppet theatre at **Ca' Rezzonico** (*see page 72*). It is also easy to entice them into the **Doge's Palace** by taking the 'secret itinerary' through its prisons, secret passages and torture chambers. At the **Scuola di San Giorgio degli Schiavoni** (*see page 123*), Carpaccio's fairytale-like *Cycle of St George* with its scenes of dragons, knights, princesses and lions will delight even young children.

Churches

Climbing church towers is one of the highlights of a visit to Venice. The best are **San Giorgio Maggiore** (*see page 138*) and the **Campanile di San Marco** (*see page 92*). Time your ascent to coincide with the striking of the hour – but take earplugs at midday!

After dark

Venice goes to bed early. As a result, city nightlife is distinctly low key, with few nightclubs, discos or late-night bars. Most locals content themselves with a meal out and a twilight passeggiata *on Riva degli Schiavone or the Zattere, maybe rounding off the evening with a nightcap in a cosy bar.*

Party animals in Venice must content themselves with a handful of top-notch piano bars, some lively pubs and the occasional disco, or head across the causeway to the frenetic club scene of Mestre. Culture vultures, on the other hand, are spoilt for choice, with a wide and tempting choice of theatre, opera and musical entertainment.

Cinema

Considering Venice hosts one of Europe's leading film festivals on the Lido every summer (*see page 135*), the city has surprisingly few cinemas. The best of these are the Accademia (*Calle Contarini Corfu 1018, Dorsoduro*) and the Ritz (*Calle dei Segretaria 617, San Marco*). Both mainly show the latest international releases (dubbed into Italian), but sometimes stage original-version 'art-house' films too. In summer there is also an open-air cinema in Campo San Polo.

Classical music, opera and theatre

Even though Venice has no concert hall or opera house (until La Fenice is rebuilt), the city's wealth of musical and theatrical offerings is immense. Sadly, Venice has become a victim of its great musical tradition, churning out little other than Venetian baroque – and mostly Vivaldi at that. With tourists far outweighing local audiences, tickets are frequently overpriced and the quality of the performance suffers at times. However, for many the experience of hearing Vivaldi in Venice is a must and the concert settings are often worth visiting as much for their surroundings as the music.

Favourite venues include the Scuola Grande di San Rocco (*see pages 58–9*), the Scuola di San Giovanni Evangelista (*see page 61*), the Frari, San Stae and San Bartolomeo, and Vivaldi's own church, La Pietà (*see page 116*), with its exceptional acoustics. In summer, concerts are also staged in the garden of Ca' Rezzonico (*see page 72*) and in the courtyard of the Doge's Palace.

Despite the fire in January 1996 which utterly destroyed La Fenice, the opera company is still operating from a marquee on one of the islands in the lagoon (*see page 107*), with all proceeds going towards the restoration fund. The opera season takes place in winter, with concerts, recitals and ballet throughout the year.

Venice's principal theatre is Teatro Goldoni (*Calle Goldoni 4650b; tel: 041 5205422*). It performs works by the eponymous eighteenth-century dramatist Carlo Goldoni and other predominantly Italian classics from November to June, and is also a popular concert venue. Teatro a l'Avogaria (*Corte Zappa 1617, Dorsoduro; tel: 041 5206130*) specialises in traditional Commedia dell'Arte performances, while Teatro Toniolo in Mestre (*Palazzo Battisti; tel: 041 971666*) stages mostly contemporary plays and modern dance productions.

Casinos

Venice has been gripped by gambling fever ever since the city opened its first public gaming house, the **Ridotto in Palazzo Dandolo**, in 1638. There are two casinos in the city: the **Casino Municipale** on the Grand Canal (*Palazzo Vendramin-Calergi, Cannaregio; Oct–Mar, 1600–0230*) and the **Palazzo del Casino** on the Lido (*Lungomare Marconi; Apr–Sept, 1600–0230*). Both casinos have their own nightclubs.

Live music

For live jazz, try **Da Codroma** wine bar (*Fondamenta Briati, Dorsoduro*) on Tuesday nights or **Paradiso Perduto** (*Fondamenta della Misericordia, Cannaregio*) on Monday nights. Another popular haunt, though hardly Venetian, is the **Fiddler's Elbow Irish Pub** (*Strada Nova, Cannaregio*) on Tuesday nights, for anything from acid jazz to Latino to folk. The main venue for rock and pop concerts is the **Arena** in Verona.

Discos and clubs

There are only two discos in Venice: the large, new **Casanova Disco Café** (*see page 33*) in Cannaregio and the tiny, gay-friendly **Piccolo Mondo** (also called El Souk; *see page 81*) in Dorsoduro.

Most of the big discos and clubs are concentrated in Mestre on the mainland. **Area City** (*Via Don Tosatto 9; Sat only, 2300–0400*) is especially popular, playing commercial dance and house music, while **007** (*Via delle Industrie 32; Fri and Sat only, 2300–0400*), just ten minutes by bus from Piazzale Roma, is the nearest mainland disco to Venice, playing all the latest sounds, with the occasional live concert and guest appearances by big-name DJs.

In summer, there is a lively nightlife scene on the Lido, concentrated mainly on the seafront hotel discos, but the main nightlife focus for young Venetians is the **Lido di Jesolo**, the sprawling seaside resort on the Adriatic coast, where young Venetians boogie the night away along with all the tourists. Top venues include the **Aida** (*Via Roma Destra; June–Sept, 2300– 0500*) with a young crowd and three dance floors, and the aptly named **XS** (*Via Belgio; Sat and Sun in summer, 2300–0500*) for a weekly fix of house music.

Listings and tickets

To find out what's on and when, pick up a copy of the invaluable free booklet **Un Ospite a Venezia/A Guest in Venice** from the tourist office or your hotel, a bilingual mine of information on all Venetian sights and services. For further information, **Venice Pocket** – another excellent, free booklet crammed with useful details – is available quarterly from the tourist office, which also produces a glossy free monthly magazine called **Leo**, containing informative features on city life and a handy pull-out section of events for that month. For specific nightlife listings, buy a copy of the monthly magazine *Venezia News* at a news-stand; for information on the entire Veneto region, check the local papers: both *Il Gazzettino* and *La Nuova Venezia* detail all the major theatrical and musical events.

Some events can be booked at the tourist offices or through one of the many travel and tourist agencies around the city, but usually you can purchase tickets at the box office immediately prior to performances. However, in summer and throughout the year for major concerts and first-night productions, it's better to reserve your ticket in advance to avoid disappointment. Expect to visit the box office in person, as telephone bookings are rarely taken.

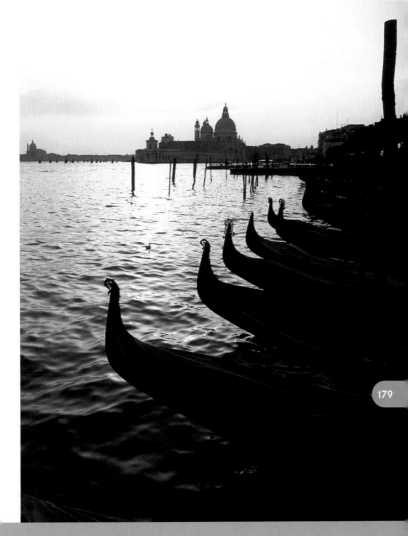

Practical
information

Practical information

Airports

There are direct flights to Venice from most major European cities, but no direct intercontinental flights. The city is served by two airports: **Marco Polo** (*tel: 041 2609260*), 10km (6 miles) north of the city on the mainland, receives both domestic and international flights; and **Treviso** (*tel: 0422 315111*), a smaller airport 30km (19 miles) north of Venice, caters mostly for charter flights. There is also a small airport at **Verona** (*tel: 045 8095666*) which accepts both charter and scheduled flights, and provides easy access to the Veneto, Lake Garda and the Dolomites.

Most visitors to Venice land at Marco Polo airport. Daily scheduled flights are operated here by **Alitalia**, the national carrier. In addition, European low-cost airlines such as British Airways' subsidiary company **Go** are currently offering bargain-rate charter flights (*for further information, call Alitalia on 041 2581333 and Go – in the UK – on 0845 6054321*).

Entry formalities

All visitors to Italy require a valid passport. Visas are not required for UK, Eire, American, Canadian, Australian, New Zealand or other EU nationals for stays of under three months. Nationals of most other countries will need a **visa**, which must be obtained from your nearest Italian embassy or consulate before you travel. Within three days of arrival, all visitors to Italy have to present their passport and register with the police. Most visitors have this formality taken care of by their hotels when they check in.

Customs regulations

Goods bought duty- and tax-paid in Italy can be brought into the UK without limit, if they are for personal consumption or to be given as gifts. The current allowances for goods bought duty free by non-EU visitors are: 400 cigarettes or 200 small cigars or 50 cigars or 250g of tobacco; 1 litre of spirits (over 22% alcohol) or 2 litres of fortified wine or 4 litres wine; 250ml cologne or 50ml of perfume.

Getting to/from Marco Polo airport

The most spectacular entry (but not the cheapest) from the airport into

Venice is by boat. The *motoscafo* water-bus leaves at hourly intervals and takes just over an hour to get to **San Marco**, with stops at **Murano**, the **Lido**, **Arsenale** and **Zattere**. Tickets are available from the ATVO office close to the exit of the arrivals hall. Water-taxis take 20 minutes to San Marco from the airport, but will cost a lot more.

The cheapest, but least scenic, route into Venice is by bus. Blue ATVO airport coaches coincide with most incoming and outgoing scheduled flights and shuttle passengers directly to and from **Piazzale Roma**. Cheaper still, but stopping along the way, is the public orange ACTV bus (No 5), which departs every 30 minutes and takes approximately 25 minutes to get to Piazzale Roma. From here, you can catch a water-bus to the nearest landing-stage to your hotel.

And remember: the key to successful transfers is to travel light. Unlike most holiday destinations, there is no door-to-door taxi service, and although there are porters at the airport to help you with your luggage, you will invariably have to hump it in and out of boats at some time during your stay, not to mention drag it through the maze of alleyways and over countless bridges to and from your hotel.

Disabled travellers

Venice does not cater well for travellers with disabilities. Few public buildings have disabled facilities, the crowded alleyways are uneven and often too narrow for wheelchair access, there are 400 hump-backed bridges to contend with, and many churches have steps to negotiate.

However, in recent years an effort has been made to improve facilities. The Tourist Office now offers maps of the city highlighting itineraries and areas accessible to wheelchair-bound visitors, as well as indicating specially adapted public toilets and the handful of bridges with wheelchair ramps (all in the **San Marco district**). Some bridges also have special chair-lifts for wheelchair users, operated by special keys, also available from the Tourist Office.

Surprisingly, perhaps, public transport is easier for disabled travellers than in many cities, as most *vaporetti* and *motonavi* (but not *motoscafi*; *see page 15*) have large, flat decks which lie flush with the quayside, making it moderately straightforward to get aboard. Disabled access is guaranteed on routes 1, 3, 4, 6, 12, 14 and 82, but rush hour is best avoided.

183

Tourist offices

Venice's Azienda di Promozione Turistica (APT) tourist information offices can be found at **Piazza San Marco 71** (*tel: 041 5208964; open: Mon–Sat 0930–1530*), in the arrivals hall at **Marco Polo airport** (*tel: 041 5415887; open: Mon–Sat 0930–1530*) and at the railway station, **Ferrovia Santa Lucia** (*tel: 041 5298727; open: Mon–Sat 0900–1900*). During summer months, there is another office at **Gran Viale Santa Maria Elisabetta 6a** on the Lido (*tel: 041 5265721; open: Mon–Sat 1000–1300*).

Italian State Tourist Boards (ENIT) abroad

Canada: 1 Place Ville Marie, Suite 1914, Montreal, Quebec H3B 2C3. Tel: 514 8667667.
UK: 1 Princess Street, London W1R 8AY. Tel: 020 7355 1557.
US: 630 5th Avenue, Suite 1565, New York, NY 10111. Tel: 212 245 4822.

Maps

Tourist offices will provide you with a free city map, also detailing **Murano**, **Burano**, **Torcello** and the **Lido**. For up-to-date public transport maps and information, pick up a free ACTV timetable from their main office in Piazzale Roma, or at any of the larger *vaporetto* piers.

Climate

Summers are usually warm and sunny and winters mild, but with so much water about, the high levels of humidity can make hot days especially muggy and oppressive, and wintery days bitterly cold. Spring and autumn are generally mild, with **November** and **March** the rainiest months. The hottest months (and the most crowded) are **July** and **August**.

Time

Italy is on Central European time (one hour ahead of GMT in winter, two hours in summer).

Health

No vaccinations are required to enter Italy unless you are coming from a known infected area, but bring **mosquito repellent** and **sunscreen** in the summer.

Should you require medical treatment, EU residents are entitled to the same care as an Italian as long as you have the correct forms – an **E111** for British citizens, available through post offices in the UK. These

forms cover essential medical treatment, although you will have to pay prescription charges and a percentage of the cost of medicines. They do not provide cover for holiday cancellation, nor do they provide repatriation in case of illness. **Private medical insurance** is therefore also advisable, as is, of course, **full travel insurance**.

Canadian citizens are also covered by a reciprocal arrangement between the Italian and Canadian governments. Other non-EU visitors should take out personal health insurance to cover every eventuality.

If you need to visit a doctor, take the E111 form and a passport to the local health office (**Unità Sanitaria Locale**), who will direct you to a doctor. For emergency treatment, call **113** for an ambulance or go to the nearest hospital casualty department (*pronto soccorso*). In central Venice, this is likely to be the **Ospedale Civile** (*Campo Santi Giovanni e Paolo; tel: 041 5230000*), which is also accessible by water-taxi.

Dental treatment is expensive in Italy, but should be covered by private medical insurance. A list of *dentisti medici* can be found in the yellow pages of the telephone directory.

Pharmacies (*farmacia*) can easily be recognised by a red or green cross sign. They provide a wide range of prescribed and over-the-counter medicines and drugs and can also offer medical advice on minor ailments.

Tap water is generally safe to drink, unless marked *acqua non potabile*, but as Venetians generally prefer to drink mineral water, bottled water is widely available.

Currency

Italian currency is the *lira*, abbreviated to 'L'. Notes come in denominations of L1 000, L2 000, L5 000, L10 000, L50 000 and L100 000. There are L5, L10, L50, L100, L200 and L500 coins, and L200 telephone tokens (*gettoni*) can also be used as coins. All those zeros can be confusing for first-timers, so make sure you check carefully if you don't want to be short-changed. Credit cards (*carte di credito*) are accepted in most places, but cash is still the preferred method of payment.

Tipping

A 10–15 per cent service charge (*servizio*) is usually included in restaurant bills, but waiters expect a small tip on top. It is normal to leave L100 or L200 on the counter when buying drinks at the bar. Keep L1 000 or L2 000 notes handy for tipping chambermaids, theatre usherettes, cloakroom attendants and porters, and also for custodians or sacristans who open up churches or museums out of hours.

Safety and security

Venice is reputedly the safest city in Europe. Nevertheless, it pays to take the usual precautions. Don't carry more cash than you need, and beware of pickpockets, especially around **St Mark's Square**, the **Rialto Bridge** and other crowded places.

Opening times

Banks: Mon–Fri 0800–1400. Outside banking hours, money exchange facilities are available at Marco Polo airport, Santa Lucia railway station and major bank branches.

Businesses: Mon–Fri 0900–1400 and 1600–1900.

Cafés: From early morning (0700 or 0800) until late (typically 2400, although some café-bars stay open until 0100/0200).

Churches: Mon–Sat 0900–1200, 1630–1900; Sun 1500–1700.

Museums: Museum times vary and many close on Mondays. See individual entries for details, and phone ahead to avoid disappointment.

Pharmacies: Mon–Fri 0900–1230, 1600–2000; Sat 0900–1200, but local rota systems ensure at least one pharmacy in the area is open 24 hours a day. Check the rosters posted on the doors, in the local newspapers or in the booklet *Un Ospite a Venezia*.

Post offices: Mon–Fri 0800–1330. Some also open on Saturday morning. The main post office (*ufficio postale*), at Salizzada del Fontego dei Tedesche, 5554 San Marco (near the Rialto Bridge), is open Mon–Sat 0815–1900 (*tel: 041 2717111*).

Restaurants and bars: From 1230–1500 and 1930–2230, but this may vary slightly from one establishment to the next. Bars stay open later in the evening, typically until 0100 or 0200. They all have a statutory closing day (*riposo settimanale*) every week, and many close for annual holidays during August.

Shops: Mon–Sat 0900/1000–1230/1300, 1600–1930 (1700–2000 in summer), although some of the larger stores and tourist shops stay open all day. Most shops are closed on Sundays, and many shops remain closed on Monday mornings (except food shops, which close on Wednesday afternoons).

Tourist offices: The main APT Tourist Office at St Mark's Square is open Mon–Sat 0930–1530.

Public holidays

1 Jan	New Year's Day
6 Jan	Epiphany
Mar/Apr	Easter Monday
25 Apr	Liberation Day and St Mark's Day (patron saint of Venice)
1 May	Labour Day
15 Aug	Assumption
1 Nov	All Saints' Day
8 Dec	Immaculate Conception
25 Dec	Christmas Day
26 Dec	St Stephen's Day

Telephones

Public phones are indicated by a **red or yellow sign**. They can be found in most of the main squares, at most *vaporetto* piers, in some bars and restaurants, and in special offices called *centri telefoni* where you speak first and pay later. Phones accept L100, L200 and L500 coins, tokens (*gettoni*) worth L200 and phone cards (*schede telefoniche*), available from post offices, tobacconists and certain bars in L5 000, L10 000 and L15 000 denominations. Remember to break off the card's small marked corner before use. Some phones also accept credit cards.

Emergency telephone numbers

National Police (*Polizia di Stato*) / General SOS:	**113**
City Police (*Carabinieri*):	**112**
Fire (*Vigili del Fuoco*):	**115**
Ambulance (*Ambulància*):	**118**
Hospital (*Ospedale Civile*):	**041 5230000**

International dialling codes

From Venice to UK 0044, USA and Canada 001, Australia 0061, New Zealand 0064, Ireland 00353, South Africa 0027.

From outside Italy to Venice, dial 0039 for Italy then 041 for Venice.

Cheap rate for calls is Mon–Sat 2200–0800 and all day Sunday.

Toilets

Public toilets are **few and far between** in Venice, mostly near the major tourist sites (and at

Piazzale Roma and the railway station), and you have to pay the attendant in order to use them. Alternatively, most bars, hotels, fast-food outlets and department stores let you use their facilities, although they probably won't be as clean as the public toilets, and they won't necessarily provide paper.

Electricity

The electric current is **220 volts AC**, and sockets generally have either two or three round pins. British visitors require an adaptor plug, US visitors a voltage transformer.

Websites

www.venetia.it
The city's official site – useful for general information, including museum times.

www.meetingvenice.it
Detailed information on where to stay, what to do, where to eat and other useful information, including *vaporetto* timetables, a calendar of events and live weather reports.

www.iuav.unive.it
Multilingual website with a staggering number of Venice links, including information on saving the city from sinking and walk tours.

www.goitaly.about.com
Covers sightseeing, shopping, restaurants and accommodation and even has a Venice chat-line.

www.virtualvenice.net
Everything from late-night bars and camping to buying sexy underwear and getting married in Venice.

Reading

Travel memoirs

Venice by Jan Morris – an evocative, impressionistic account of the city.

Venetian Life by W D Howells – portraying the lives of ordinary Venetians before the advent of mass tourism.

Venice – a Literary Companion by Ian Littlewood – a compendium of literary comment and anecdote.

History and art

The Stones of Venice by John Ruskin – an influential study of Venetian art history.

Venice – a Biography of a City by Christopher Hibbert.

Palaces and Churches along the Grand Canal by Umberto Franzoi.

Palaces of Venice and *Villas of the Veneto* by Peter Lauritzen.

Classical literature, fiction and biography

The Merchant of Venice by William Shakespeare.

Memoirs by Giacomo Casanova.

The Wings of the Dove by Henry James – a Venetian melodrama.

Death in Venice by Thomas Mann – the most famous novel set in the city.

The Anonymous Venetian by Donna Leon – a tourist-orientated thriller.

Dead Lagoon by Michael Dibdin – a subtle detective story.

189

Index

191

Editorial, design and production credits

Project management: Dial House Publishing

Series editor: Christopher Catling

Proof-reader: Gill Colver

Series and cover design: Trickett & Webb Limited

Cover artwork: Wenham Arts

Text layout: Wenham Arts

Map work: Polly Senior Cartography

Repro and image setting: Z2 Repro, Thetford, Norfolk, UK

Printed and bound by: Artes Graficas ELKAR S. Coop., Bilbao, Spain

Acknowledgements

We would like to thank Paul Murphy (pages 158, 159, 162 and 163) and John Heseltine (all the remainder) for the photographs used in this book, to whom the copyright belongs.